Power Without Permission

Real Stories & Practical Tools to Quiet Impostor Syndrome and Lead with Your Brilliance

Andreas Pettersson

With contributing stories from
Martha Chrisander, Julie Stone, Michele Jewett, Kana Waanders, Cheryl Strizelka, Stephanie Hammerwold, Cindy Chang, Marlene Braga, Marina St. Cyr, Alyssa Trenkamp, Janne Jakobsen, Carolina Hernandez, and Ryanna Hammond

Copyright © 2025 Leaders ADAPT LLC

All rights reserved.

No part of this publication may be reproduced, distributed, or transmitted in any form. This includes photocopying, recording, or any electronic or mechanical method, without the prior written permission of the author, except in the case of brief quotations embodied in critical reviews and certain other noncommercial uses permitted by copyright law.

Printed in the United States of America.

First paperback edition 2025

Cover design by Adrian Morgan

ISBN-13: 979-8-218-77415-8

Power Without Permission

Real Stories & Practical Tools to Quiet Impostor Syndrome and Lead with Your Brilliance

Andreas Pettersson

With contributing stories from
Martha Chrisander, Julie Stone, Michele Jewett, Kana Waanders, Cheryl Strizelka, Stephanie Hammerwold, Cindy Chang, Marlene Braga, Marina St. Cyr, Alyssa Trenkamp, Janne Jakobsen, Carolina Hernandez, and Ryanna Hammond

To my mother, Karin, my first teacher in the art of life and leadership.

This book is a declaration of love to you. Long before the world caught up, you proved that the most transformative leaders lead with both courage and compassion—a truth that guides everything I share in these pages.

With all my love and gratitude,
Andreas Pettersson

"The brain dies twice. First when you stop evolving. Second when your heart stops beating. The most fulfilled people time both instances in the same second."
— *M.M. Sjo*

AMOR FATI

Table of Contents

Preface
Section I: My Story & Perspective
Chapter 1: Andreas Pettersson — 21
ADAPT Framework — 39
What Is a Leader? — 41
Section II: Awareness: *See Your Potential in the Rough Stone*
Chapter 2: Overcoming Impostor Syndrome — 51
Chapter 3: Cultivating Self-Awareness — 75
Chapter 4: Developing Emotional Intelligence — 91
Chapter 5: Overcoming the Fear of Judgment — 105
Section III: Direction & Action: *Locate and Make the Initial Cuts*
Chapter 6: Navigating Power Dynamics and Office Politics — 121
Chapter 7: Setting Boundaries and Commanding Respect — 139
Chapter 8: Building Your Strategic Network — 155
Chapter 9: Taking Action — 171
Chapter 10: Developing Leadership Presence — 185
Section IV: Purpose & Transformation: *Emerge as a Polished Diamond*
Chapter 11: Leading with Purpose and Vision — 203
Chapter 12: Overcoming Gender Discrepancies in the Workplace — 217
Chapter 13: Empowering the Next Generation of Female Leaders — 233
Section V: Unlock Your Full Potential
Conclusion — 255
So, What's Next? — 259
Meet The Authors — 261
Companion Discussion Guide — 269
Acknowledgements — 273
References — 277

Preface

I know what you're thinking. You picked up a book for women and saw a male author. Maybe you rolled your eyes or thought, "How could a middle-aged white man have anything to say about women when he has never experienced, and could never experience, what we go through?" I get it—and I promise I'm not here to explain your experience to you. I'm here to share with you what remarkable women have taught me, and to highlight the competence you've always possessed but may have been conditioned to doubt.

Although I cannot step into your shoes, I can understand your shoes and empathize. And, to take this metaphor further (because I love metaphors), in a society that tries to scuff up or stomp on your shoes, I want to shine them. Or, better yet, help you acquire a new and better pair.

In other words, I don't want to live in a world where men are the only leaders—where boardrooms echo with the same voices, same instincts, and same approaches, decade after decade. Why? Because when leadership is shaped by only one ideology, everyone loses.

Across every industry, there is a lack of empathy, emotional intelligence, and intuition—qualities predominantly associated with women that get overlooked because they don't fit the narrow mold of what we've historically celebrated as "strong leadership." If the world continues as is, we'll keep building systems that serve only a few—typically a few white males—and harm everybody else.

That's why we need more women at the table—not simply to create balance or fairness, but because women are brilliant in their own right and necessary for us to establish a better future. That being said, I would never hire anyone just because of gender. I don't believe in just checking a box. But I do believe in the brain, the heart, the soul. I believe in what people are capable of, and that applies to anyone, regardless of gender, race, ethnicity, sexual orientation, religion, and so on.

Now, reading this, some women still might not be convinced, perhaps feeling indifferent or exclaiming with enraged fists, "Women don't need help from men!" No joke, I've actually been verbally attacked by women for—of all things—helping women reach higher executive positions. I know, it sounds baffling. And that kind of reaction, the war between male and female, masculine and feminine, is part of the larger issue.

I don't agree with the patriarchal way. Likewise, I don't agree with the belief that women are better than men, or that any gender should be *more* powerful than the other. To me, we are all equal, yet different, and have unique skills. If you're unsure about that, just look at anything in nature. In every thriving ecosystem, both male and female exist in complementary roles. It's not sameness that creates and multiplies life, it's differences working in tandem. And the same goes for leadership.

The most equipped leaders possess a sophisticated balance between emotional intelligence and logical intelligence. In some cases, that's women; likewise, in other cases, that's men. If we value one gender over the other, we cripple our own potential as a species. You would think this is self-explanatory, but in a world of chaos, division, and emphasis on "the other," a harmonious perspective like mine seems to get misunderstood time and time again. Sure, it might be easier to pretend we live in a black-and-white world, but the reality is, everything is gray and complex, and it's time we step into that because that's where truth, innovation, and real transformation occur.

I could ramble on about this, but you get the gist. Plus, you'll have plenty of time to get to know my perspective over the course of this book. What matters now is telling you what you'll find within these pages: tools, lessons, activities, and stories—not only from me, but from thirteen remarkable women I've mentored, worked with, learned from, and/or been mentored by in the business world.

This book isn't based on academic research or theoretical frameworks. It's built from real conversations, real coaching sessions, and real transformations I've witnessed over fifteen years of working with women who couldn't always see their own brilliance. The women who share their stories here aren't case studies—they're teachers who helped me recognize patterns I could never have seen alone. Their insights, alongside my own, are here to help you rewire your mindset and create transformation in your personal and professional life—whether you're just starting out, leading a company, or building your own venture. And men—should you happen to be reading this—you can learn something from this book too. Not only by applying these tools and lessons to your own life, but by utilizing what you learn to uplift the women around you, strengthen workplaces, and spark greater innovation.

I am currently the CEO of my own business, Leaders ADAPT LLC, and I once had a successful exit as a CEO in tech. Through my fifteen years of business and leadership experience, along with forty-plus years of enlightening life experiences—being raised poor by a single mother in a small town in Sweden, having a soul-sucking factory job at age nineteen, losing my father as a young adult, living with undiagnosed ADHD, raising three sons with my wife, and having a near-death experience—I've curated the ultimate framework (I call it ADAPT, and you'll hear about it soon) that I've sworn by for fifteen years to help both women and men unlock their full potential.

And at the heart of all this is the title of this book: *Power Without Permission*. I know that phrase may spark different interpretations. For me, it reflects a simple but radical truth: you already have what it takes to lead. For too long, women have been told—by culture, by systems, by expectation—to wait for approval before stepping into positions of influence. They've been taught to overachieve, over-prepare, and still feel unworthy until someone else deems them "ready."

Power Without Permission is about a mindset shift—from doubt to capability, from hesitation to action. It's about quieting the inner critic, breaking free from impostor syndrome, and remembering that authority doesn't come only from a job title, a degree, or anyone else's validation. It comes from within—from your lived experience, your emotional intelligence, your vision, and your courage to show up as yourself.

So as you move through the chapters ahead, I invite you to read with this mindset: you don't need permission. You never did. The power is already yours. Everything you'll read here is rooted in that belief—and in the lessons and love of my greatest teacher, my Swedish mother, Karin.

Section I: My Story & Perspective

Chapter 1: Andreas Pettersson

"There is no greater agony than bearing an untold story inside you."
— *Maya Angelou*

Before I can take you on this book's journey, I need to begin with my story—who I am and what shaped me—because any quality leader knows that leadership begins with honesty and vulnerability. Leadership isn't about standing on a pedestal; it's about standing with those you aim to lead, understanding their struggles, and showing them that, just like you, they can rise above their challenges.

While some stories start with love or loss, mine began with survival. I was born in Sweden in 1980 to a single mother who worked long hours at a daycare to make ends meet. Some months, when she was extremely low on money, we could only afford to buy pasta and potatoes in bulk to stretch across every meal. I only owned a few shirts and one pair of jeans, which I had to learn to wash myself. One time, I remember tearing and ruining a pair of jeans, and it really upset my mom—but at the time, I didn't understand why. By the age of six, I was leaving home alone, walking home alone, cooking for myself, and cleaning up after myself, since my mother was working, doing everything she could to keep us going.

My father was a ghost who would float in once every three months, and just as quickly as he appeared, he would vanish. Each time he visited, he came with an excuse for staying away so long. He had extended work on the road as a salesman. He borrowed money from people and had to pay them back. He was working two to three jobs and simply didn't have time to come home.

I did not bat an eye at any of his tales until I was thirteen, when my girlfriend at the time asked me why my father was never home.

"He's working," I said—but this time, when it came out of my mouth, I questioned it.

I approached my mom later that day. "Why do I rarely see my dad? Is he really on the road or is something else going on?"

"I don't know, Andreas," she replied, her shoulders shrugging.

And she was telling the truth. She really didn't know either, I think. He was lying to both of us. I ended up finding out that he had another family, that I had a half-brother and a half-sister, who I later met on my father's deathbed when I was 23. I felt so stupid. How could I have been tricked so easily for so many years?

I have no doubt that these early experiences shaped how I viewed leaders and authority. I had a father, but no prominent male figure. My mother served as both my mother and father figure. And honestly, there weren't many traditional families in the area we lived in either. Most of my friends had single moms growing up, so even at their houses I saw really strong women and mothers. Plus, beyond what I saw at home, there were plenty of prominent female figures around me, on TV, and in politics: Margaret Thatcher, Karin Söder, Mona Sahlin, Gro Harlem Brundtland, Marjorie Scardino, and the Queen of England, to name a few.

Though, as a kid growing up in Sweden in the 1990s, our idea of female power went far beyond queens, politicians, and CEOs. We all grew up with Pippi Longstocking—on TV, in school, in movies. Created by Astrid Lindgren (also one of the most influential women in Swedish cultural history), Pippi wasn't just a fictional character. She was a force of nature: strong, fearless, clever, and unapologetically independent. She challenged every adult, defied every expectation, and fought—often literally—against male authority figures. And none of us fans ever questioned her right to do so. In fact, we admired her for it. That's the kind of imagination we had as a nation.

It's no wonder, then, why we grew up believing that female leadership was natural and normal—and even expected. I never felt that influence or authority was tied to a specific gender, or one gender more than the other. And that is one thing that absolutely shocked me when I later came to the United States. The gender gap in politics, business, leadership—

everywhere—was glaringly prominent compared to my European upbringing. According to the most recent Global Gender Gap report, Sweden ranks fifth in the world, while the U.S. ranks forty-third (Ruggeri, 2023).

The most prominent female figure of all, though, was of course my mother. She is no doubt the reason why I valued women so highly from a young age. Beyond her incredible qualities—warm, firm, caring, passionate, curious—she taught me vital lessons and morals. For one, I grew up with people from various religions, ethnicities, races, sexual orientations, etc., and from day one she taught me that those external things don't matter. What matters is every individual's uniqueness. She would say in Swedish something like, "Everyone's a diamond in the rough. You just have to find that thing in everyone that makes them valuable." In other words, what she taught me to see was the soul—what was on the inside.

Whenever there was a new kid in school, she would encourage me to be the first one to welcome them and befriend them because they were in a new environment. Those moments with new kids taught me empathy—to see life beyond my own view. And I'll never forget when we would spend our weekends asking for money for the Red Cross to send to people in need in developing countries. We would be out of money halfway through the month, eating the same thing every day (potatoes or pasta), and yet there we were shaking cups, asking for coins and bills for others. One time I even asked her, "Why don't we keep this money for ourselves?" The look she gave me was one of bewilderment, as if that were absolutely impossible. "We have something right now. Some people have nothing. It's the right thing to do."

Though we lived in a lower- to mid-income area (by Sweden's standards, it was still fairly nice and safe due to our welfare system), we were only a few blocks away from a richer area of the city, so I ended up in school with children who had a much better socioeconomic status than I did. For example, schoolmates' families that had both mothers and fathers could afford bi-yearly vacations to ski or go to exotic countries. A lot of my interest in potentially obtaining college degrees came from witnessing those peers and their families, and the lives they created for themselves through education. I didn't see many people from my neighborhood eagerly pursue schooling. My mother had tried going to a higher education program when I was little, and I remember sitting in on some classes with her, but it was too hard having a young son and no money. She had to focus on her daycare job and make side money by cutting hair and cleaning houses.

But despite my drive to succeed, school didn't work out for me the first time around. I had undiagnosed ADHD and didn't know how to cope with it. My mother would tell me, "Do what makes you happy." Though this is good advice, to a young teenager, that meant not pursuing school. In high school, I did not have an attendance rate above 30%. I couldn't control my brain. I'm not kidding when I say that every morning, my mom would take me out of bed an hour early, and we would go for a run to try to help me slow down—control my body to control my mind. And she constantly studied with me on the move. Since I couldn't concentrate, we would walk around and talk while she read papers aloud and quizzed me. I just couldn't do it. I couldn't focus. Plus, I lied to her about school and got caught a few times, which pushed her to try to help me even more.

I ended up failing out of high school and moving with my girlfriend at the time to a small village in the Swedish countryside, with maybe twenty people total. She was really happy there—it had been her dream to live in a place like that. I, on the other hand, was miserable.

I knew I needed to bring money in for us, so I started working the night shift at an industrial rubber factory about one hour from where we lived. I swear I can still smell the pungent rubber and grimy machinery. That place was where my mental health hit an all-time low. I was away from my mom, settled into a mediocre relationship, and living in a place I didn't like. I had to sleep during the day, which meant I rarely saw the sun. And I couldn't stop thinking: *This was where my life took me.* A dirty, dead-end factory job surrounded by people who complained constantly, blamed the world for their problems, had no ambition—and were drunk more often than sober.

I was one of the youngest employees and kept coming up with improvements to the machines and processes. Even though

I was earning bonuses and receiving praise, I still didn't believe in myself—because I had failed high school. I told myself I was stupid, that I would never amount to anything, and surrendered to the belief that this was simply how my life would be.

One night, I was sitting there, running four machines at once, when I zoned out and started imagining driving my car into a tree at rapid speed to end my life. I'm not sure how long I was lost in that dark daydream, but it must have been at least half an hour. Suddenly, alarms were going off, and I snapped out of it. I looked around the dull, gray room at all the lifeless mechanical things around me.

"What the fuck are you doing, Andreas?" I asked myself. The reality of my mental state was disconcerting. "You're not like these people." My mother's voice rang in my ears: *Do what makes you happy*. Clearly, this wasn't it. I stood up, quit on the spot, and never set foot in that factory again.

The fear drove me to shift my life immediately. I left that area and redid high school. Determined not to waste my life, I graduated in two years with top grades. I wasn't sure what I wanted to do yet, but I had always been interested in software development and had dabbled in computer stuff as a kid.

A childhood friend of mine was going to college nearby for a computer program, so I decided to visit him at his school. I was curious about how he was doing and what the program was like—he'd always been wicked smart growing up.

I'll never forget the conversation we had outside of his dorm. He was leaning against the wall, smoking a cigarette, when he told me he was failing and would have to switch to an easier major.

"Failing?" I said, shocked.

"Yeah." He took a long drag. "So what are you going to do? I heard you went back to high school."

"I was actually thinking of applying here… to the software engineering program you're in."

He started laughing. "Andreas, there is no way. There is no fucking way you have the smarts or intelligence to do this."

Some friend.

Immediately, I thought, *Fuck you.* But I didn't say it out loud. I just shrugged my shoulders, thinking, *I'm going to do it, and I'm going to pass.*

Not only did I get into that program, I graduated on time—with great grades—as one of just four students out of a twenty-six-person cohort. I went straight into a Master's in Software Engineering, totaling four and a half years of post-high school study.

My schedule during those years was intense. I worked forty hours from Friday through Sunday as a waiter at a restaurant owned by two sisters, one of whose boyfriends was in my college program. From Monday through Thursday, I studied and took classes.

There was one woman in my class, a single mom with two kids, who constantly struggled with the workload. I helped her with assignments whenever I could, knowing how hard it must've been for her. In many ways, she reminded me of my own mother, so I had a soft spot for her. I didn't know it at the time, but this experience marked the beginning of a pattern that would emerge throughout my life.

I started working in 2007 as a consultant, and even though I had degrees under my belt, I still hadn't addressed my deeply embedded self-worth issues—rooted in my father's absence, initially failing high school, and struggling with ADHD. In the corporate world, I quickly realized that most of the people around me played golf and came from families where parents were lawyers and doctors. I felt out of place, like my life had been very different from theirs, and that only exacerbated my lack of self-worth and impostor syndrome.

Three months into my consultant job, we had a major customer issue with our biggest client, and there was a meeting about it. Every male developer was in the room, along with my manager, myself, one woman who worked in tech writing, and a second woman in customer support. The two women were advocating for the emotional side of the customer experience, while all the men—six or seven of them—were focused solely on logic and technical aspects, disregarding what the women were saying about the customer's pain points and needs. I was incredibly frustrated, my whole body shaking with irritation toward my male colleagues.

"Andreas, do you have something to say?" my manager finally asked.

"You're all idiots," I said. "You're missing the point that is so obviously clear. Are you blind? Listen to what the women in the room are saying! We're completely ignoring the emotional needs of the customer."

The women nodded. "Yeah, Andreas gets it."

All the men disagreed—except my manager. After the meeting, he called me in and asked for a full outline on how to elevate the product. The material I gave him became the direction we followed, and it solved the issue. A week later, he came to me and said, "I want you to become a product manager."

Now, I know how this might sound. The male who spoke up got promoted. *What gives? What about the women?* Well, for one, neither of them were in the same department as me, so they weren't eligible for the role I stepped into. But secondly, that moment marked a turning point for me as a leader. I saw how often women are dismissed—even when they're right—and how critical it is to use your voice to amplify and validate others. The women's insights were sharp, emotionally intelligent, and 100% accurate. I truly listened to them. I believe that's why I got promoted over the other developers, all of whom were male and had ignored what the women were saying.

It was actually at that company where I also met my wife and the mother of my children, Vesna. We fell in love, traveled together, all those things. Our birthdays are only a few weeks apart, so when I turned thirty, we threw a joint birthday party and invited everyone we loved. Only it wasn't just a joint birthday—we got married right beforehand and showed up in our wedding outfits, surprising everyone with the news. A few months later, I left that job, but Vesna stayed a little while longer. (More on Vesna in a bit.)

Within six months at my new company, the CEO saw my potential. Believing I was a diamond in the rough, he got me into a leadership training program, which became one of the most pivotal experiences of my life. Around that time, I also wanted to go back to school to get an MBA. A male peer at my company egoically wished me luck: "I finished an MBA in two years while working full-time. I bet you couldn't do that, Andreas. You'd fail. I dare you to even try."

Not only did I try, I earned my MBA in one year, while working full-time and participating in the leadership program, though it required sacrificing time with my wife and sleeping exactly four to five hours every night (plus the occasional power nap at a desk or on a couch).

One particular exercise in that program stands out in my memory. We were asked to give a speech on something that frustrated us. It was called the "beer crate speech," a throwback to when beer crates were used in Denmark to hold glass bottles. The crate would be turned upside down, and you'd stand on it to speak. The challenge was that you weren't allowed to move and had to stay completely still for ten minutes. I didn't struggle with the speech itself, but with what came after.

The leadership psychologist and the peer group would spend the next few hours discussing what they observed about you. You weren't allowed to speak during this process. You just had to sit in silence, your back turned to the group, looking out of the window, while you heard what others truly thought of you—whether you were prepared for it or not. It didn't take long for the conversation to veer from surface-level observations to much deeper, more painful analyses as the psychologist pushed the group to dig deeper, deeper, deeper.

At some point, the psychologist said something like, "I think Andreas grew up without a father. I think he doesn't understand what a father figure is, or what male authority is. And I think he is a male authority now, but he doesn't understand how to wield that role—how to view it in a healthy way."

Hearing that was like a punch to the gut. I didn't even know how to react. I just stared out the window, watching the wind and rain, unable to say a word. The others' comments followed—breaking down my persona, my behavior, the way I interacted with others. What they were saying was true. I felt rage toward men. I often challenged male authority whenever I could, wearing my "brilliant asshole" persona like armor. The man I was subconsciously fighting was my dead father—and because of that, the biggest fight of all was with myself. I couldn't fully grasp what was happening, and the internal conflict became overwhelming. I began to cry. And once the floodgates opened, the tears didn't stop.

After what felt like an eternity, the session ended. I didn't speak to anyone. I quickly got in my car and drove home, mentally and emotionally drained. My head was spinning from the realizations I was having. I didn't know what a father figure was. I didn't know what "masculine" authority meant, and I didn't respect it. I just saw authority as authority, regardless of gender (though most authority figures I'd ever seen were women). Suddenly, I was seeing myself differently, seeing my role in the world differently—like I was a foreigner inside my own body and mind. I couldn't take it. No joke, I fell asleep as soon as I got home at 5:00 p.m. and didn't wake up until 10:00 a.m. the following Saturday morning.

To make things even more difficult, not long after that—on the same night I turned in my Master's Thesis for my MBA—Vesna plopped a positive pregnancy test in front of me on the desk and said something that felt both surreal and terrifying: "Congratulations, Andreas. You're going to be a father."

A father.
A father.
It echoed in my brain. What?

The internal battle only worsened. I didn't know how to be a father. What if I... became *my* father? Some part of me knew that could never happen. I would never cheat on my wife. I would never leave my child. I would never disappear the way he did. Still, the reality of having to step into another male authority role—this time for my child—was overwhelming.

It kicked me into gear. I knew I had to face myself and work on my mindset. I sought deeper work with the leadership psychologist, and we began to talk for hours—unpacking my past, my trauma, my beliefs. I had a laundry list of issues, and I'm sure some of them will sound familiar to you too:

1. Despite achieving great things at this stage in my career—including multiple promotions—I had impostor

syndrome and was an insecure overachiever. I constantly felt like I was "faking it".
2. I didn't see myself as fully worthy of the success I'd attained because I had initially failed high school.
3. My father had been gone for nearly a decade, and I still hadn't fully grieved the loss of him—or the loss of never truly having him.
4. Whenever I accomplished something, I wouldn't celebrate. Instead, I'd immediately move on to the next challenge, afraid of losing what I had and going back to where I came from. (Going back to the factory, contemplating which tree I'd run my car into.)
5. I had a hard time believing the positive things people said about me, often dismissing it as empty praise or self-serving flattery.
6. I didn't know how to set boundaries. I was always there for others and never there for myself.
7. Inside me was a deep fear of being judged. I didn't want others to see "my true self," or who I had been as a child. For the most part, I hid where I came from.
8. I felt like I had no mentors, peers, or friends I could relate to, which made me feel both alone and lonely in my struggles.
9. There was no clear life path or plan I was following. Honestly, I was just consumed by myriad fears.

Through this deep introspection, my leadership psychologist helped me realize that these feelings of inadequacy stemmed from a lifetime of negative feedback. I had to break down the survival mechanisms I'd developed as a child, being surrounded by people who didn't nurture or uplift me—except, of course, for my mother. Ironically, when I was young, I believed I needed to learn from the parents of my peers—lawyers, doctors, and entrepreneurs—not my mother, who I thought was naive. (Yes, I was stupid!) But through this psychological process, the truth became brilliantly clear: She was the wisest one of all.

The work with both my psychologist and mentors wasn't easy. I had to relive significant moments of my life, again and again. It was painful—but it was necessary for my growth. Over that year-and-a-half process of self-discovery, I finally began to accept that I was really smart, that I was good at my job, and that I was an effective leader. That's why I kept getting promoted, receiving bonuses, and moving into higher positions. For the first time, I truly believed I was capable, worthy, and—most importantly—a great father. I also realized that I had to stop letting fear be my biggest motivator. While it had once been helpful to get me to urgently leave the factory job, it wasn't effective in the long-term. I started embracing an abundance mindset, which enhanced my passion, my vision, and my sense of fulfillment.

Emerging from that season of deep self-work, I found myself at a turning point: no longer defined by the pain of my past, but stepping into the responsibilities of the future. So when life ushered me into the next chapter—with another child on the way, a cross-continental move, and new responsibilities—it felt like the true test of all that inner work.

In 2014, Vesna—eight months pregnant with our second child—and I, along with our 13-month-old son Leon, migrated from Sweden to the Bay Area in California with the company I'd been working for. Around that time, two female friends of mine needed support, and I gladly offered it. One was earning her bachelor's in psychology and struggled with the math-heavy research and statistics courses. I remember sitting with her for hours in my backyard, helping her memorize and understand formulas so she could pass. The other was one of the restaurant owners from my college job in Sweden. She was exiting an unhealthy relationship and was clinically depressed. I paid for her flight to the U.S., and Vesna and I helped her get back on her feet shortly after we relocated to Orange County in Southern California. At the time, I didn't realize I was developing a natural pattern of helping the women around me.

I was still working for the incubation and venture company, which was developing multiple mini-startups at the time. In 2017 around the time our third son, Nelo, was born, one of those startups spun off. It became a huge initiative so I shifted to working there. Everything between work and home blurred into one overwhelming cluster of stress. For reasons I cannot legally—or ethically—expand on, I became CEO, CFO, and CTO all at once, just as our second son, Noel, was diagnosed with moderate to severe autism.

It felt surreal—becoming CEO of a Canon-owned company at just 37, a rare achievement, during one of the most difficult periods of my personal life. Noel struggled with communication and emotional regulation, often having tantrums for hours on end. Vesna and I didn't know what to do, so we decided to divide and conquer. I would fight the battle of being CEO, while Vesna would fight the battle for Noel's future. We agreed that if we were miserable after two years, we'd move back to Sweden.

Those two years were some of the hardest of my life. Our marriage was on pause. We were coexisting more as friends—each of us focused on our son's care—while I was also dealing with the chaos of being a first-time CEO. I was responsible for managing a company tasked with hiring eighty people in a highly volatile environment. I was constantly traveling between Europe, Japan, and the U.S. I was exhausted and overwhelmed, and I'd come home to more exhaustion and overwhelm. Vesna was drained, struggling to care for herself, and blaming herself for Noel's autism struggles.

One night, after Noel had a twelve-hour tantrum, Vesna and I sat silently in bed, at our wits' end physically and psychologically.

"If you could go back in time, now knowing how difficult this would be, would you have considered terminating the pregnancy?" I asked point-blank.

Vesna began to cry. "No," she finally said. "I mean... that's my son. That's my baby. I would never, no matter how hard it gets."

"Me either," I replied. "I think we need to stop dividing and conquering. We need to fight together."

From that moment forward, we operated differently, facing our challenges side-by-side. We dove into educating ourselves about autism. We each read a stack of books, sought professional advice, and invested in intense behavioral therapy for Noel. He made tremendous progress—going from a restrictive, specialized classroom to a regular classroom with support. Today, he's still a year or two behind academically, but he's thriving: working on his speech and communication, and able to express his feelings.

Our parenting journey with Noel transformed me as a leader in ways I never expected. It taught me resilience on a whole new level. It taught me how to truly work in partnership. It taught me that everyone—including those with special needs—is unique, brilliant, and amazing in their own way.

Vesna and I were closer than ever. Our home life was stable, beautiful, and strong. I had become a confident and emotionally intelligent CEO. And that's when I was confronted with the most soul-awakening experience of all: a near-death experience.

In 2019, I was at the pool with our three sons, enjoying a sunny afternoon in Southern California. When we got home, something felt off, strange. Since I'd been out in the sun all day, I chalked it up to fatigue. But when I sat down at the kitchen table, I suddenly started profusely sweating and couldn't relax. It felt like I'd just run a marathon—my heart was pounding, and sweat was pouring from every part of my body.

My vision narrowed. I became dizzy and lightheaded. I dropped to the floor and took a few deep breaths, trying to stay calm, but my heart raced faster. My Apple Watch beeped. I looked down and a high heart rate warning popped up—it had reached the danger zone at 200 beats per minute.

I looked at Vesna. "Something isn't right," I told her. "We need to go seek medical help. Now."

We rushed to urgent care. At first, the medical staff didn't seem alarmed. They guessed it was dehydration or maybe a panic attack. But then they ran an EKG. When they saw the results, their moods drastically changed.

The doctor's face went pale. "Andreas," he said, trying to remain calm, "you're about to have a heart attack. Your heart is going to collapse. We need to get you to the ER now."

Two medical staff wheeled me to the next building over. At this point, I was still clear-headed enough to call Vesna.

"Go ahead and park. Do not come in with the kids. Stay in the car. I'll call you as soon as I'm in a room."

I was put in a room almost immediately and hooked up to machines. An alarm started blaring. They began poking me with needles and prepping the defibrillator. I was drunk on some sort of meds they'd given me.

And that's when the gravity of the situation truly set in. *What the hell is going on?* I thought.

I looked up at the doctor. "Is my heart really going to collapse… like *potential death* collapse?" I mean, what experienced doctor would even say that to a patient?

He didn't answer me. Instead, he hollered to other staff members, "We need to do something now!"

More medics rushed into the room, prepping for what looked like surgery.

Am I dying? I wondered.

I had to text Vesna if this was going to be the last thing I ever said to her. I quickly began typing: *I love you. Please stay with the kids in the car. Also, I need you to know I really fucking love you.*

Suddenly, I felt strangely calm. I set down my phone and faded out of consciousness.

The final thought I had was: *My family will be okay. I've lived a good life.*

I had come to fully accept death—satisfied with the life I'd lived, the beautiful family Vesna and I had created, and the accomplishments, both internal and external, that I had attained.

Then I woke up. The doctors had shocked my heart. I was disoriented, but I heard voices shouting around me, "He's coming through!"

I opened my eyes. I felt nauseous. I didn't know how long I had been unconscious or what exactly the medical team had done. Had they cracked open my chest? Did they insert a pacemaker? I immediately felt around my chest, but nothing seemed out of the ordinary.

The doctors informed me that I had experienced what's called supraventricular tachycardia, combined with atrial fibrillation. Essentially, my heart rate had become so erratic that it couldn't properly function. They had pumped me full of fluids and sedatives, then shocked my heart to reset it. That's how my heart's rhythm returned to normal.

I was able to leave the hospital later that day. It turns out it's a pretty standard procedure called a cardioversion. (And as of today, I've had to do it more times than I'd want to count.)

God, was I thrilled to see my family—and terrified that I'd lose them that same night to a heart attack in my sleep. Thankfully I didn't. The following day, I called my psychologist in Denmark to process what had happened. His response shocked me to my core.

"Congratulations, Andreas," he said.

"What?" I asked, stunned.

"You accepted death early in life. You're going to wake up every day happy from now on. You'll be more resilient than 99.99% of people out there. You're unstoppable."

At the time, I had no clue what he meant. I was angry with him. How could he say that to me after what I'd just been through?

But after much processing, I've come to understand the truth in his words. I still reflect on them often.

I ended up having to undergo two heart surgeries, in addition to the handful of cardioversions I've had. With that came a powerful realization: Every day is a gift. I wake up feeling gratitude every morning because my heart is pumping and I have the privilege to say, *"I'm alive and happy."*

That brush with death gave me a keen awareness that there is no time to waste.

Not in toxic environments.

Not with toxic people.

Not with your dreams and desires.

Not with anything.

When you cut the bullshit everything becomes crystal clear—including the fact that life is not short, but long. So use it.

In 2024, I started my own coaching business, primarily working with women. I began reflecting on the highest and lowest points of my life, along with the most transformative experiences. Memories of my childhood, previous jobs, female coworkers and subordinates, the single mother from the computer program, the leadership training… they all came rushing back.

I began weaving them together like threads in a quilt, noticing the overlaps, the shared themes, the patterns that connected them all. And then it hit me:

Part of my life's purpose is to help women expand their lives—both personally and professionally.

Over the years, I've mentored and coached countless women and men from diverse backgrounds, guiding them to believe in themselves and see the potential they hadn't realized. Sometimes, I'd exert so much effort because I feared they'd regress—a fear born out of working with my son, Noel, and his autism.

I've helped lift people to the next level, over and over again. Each time I spotted potential in someone overlooked, I could hear my mother's voice reminding me that everyone has brilliance within them—worth uncovering, worth believing in.

One of my proudest moments was seeing a woman who started as an entry-level developer rise to become a rockstar team leader, managing multiple teams. She never thought she could be a leader, but I saw her potential from day one.

Another woman had been in sales. I created a new role for her in customer experience because of her uncanny ability to anticipate what customers truly wanted and needed.

Another woman: I encouraged her to stop hedging, to stop over-explaining herself, to believe in her own brilliance.

And there were countless times, in my C-level positions, when I advocated for women in the company or sought out women to lead teams. I was always working to ensure more exceptional women were at the top of companies. (You'll hear from some of them in this book).

And here's the deepest realization of all:

Just like I was indirectly fighting my father through men in authority positions, I now understand that the reason I care so deeply about helping women rise is because I'm indirectly helping my mother: the woman who had so much potential but was surrounded by people who didn't encourage her or elevate her. (Hint: Surround yourself with people who believe in you.)

My mother has been the most significant influence in my life. She's the reason I became the leader—and father—I am today. Her lessons, wisdom, and kindness have shaped me, and I strive to pass on her legacy through my work.

Now, this book is serious business. It's not a "read it and get better" quick fix. This book will challenge you. It will push you—whether you're female or male—to confront yourself. Your limitations. Your fears. Your barriers. It will be your version of leadership training. Your version of a heart attack. It will demand that you slap yourself awake to transform your life. If you're not ready for that level of honesty and self-examination, put this book down and try again in three months.

But if you are ready? Then let's begin.

ADAPT Framework

The ADAPT Framework is a methodology I have consistently applied over the past fifteen years, not only for my own personal development, but also in coaching and mentoring others. I developed this framework following the intensive leadership program in my early thirties, which significantly enhanced my self-awareness journey.

In this book, you will find the five steps of ADAPT—Awareness, Direction, Action, Purpose, and Transformation—to aid you with internal self-development, external professional development, and knowledge to go beyond yourself to make an impact in your organization and for future generations. Implementing this framework can and will revolutionize your life.

I often speak about ADAPT in the context of the "diamond in the rough" metaphor, inspired by my mother's belief that every individual has a unique, untapped potential. Like a rough diamond, business professionals and entrepreneurs often have capabilities that simply need discovery and refinement. My mission is to guide those ready to unlock and maximize their potential.

Let's break it down:

Step one: Awareness

See your potential in the rough stone. Just as a skilled artisan carefully examines a raw diamond, you must raise your self-awareness as the first step toward self-development.

Step two: Direction.

Locate your inner diamond. Like planning the perfect cut, direct your energy toward the individuals and environments that value you.

Step three: Action.

Make the initial cut. Just as a diamond cutter makes the first bold strike, take decisive action to refine your path and execute your goals.

Step four: Purpose.

Shape and refine. Just as the clarity and beauty of a diamond are enhanced with each precision cut, your purpose becomes clearer as your journey unfolds.

Step five: Transformation.

Emerge as a polished diamond. At this stage, your journey yields internal peace, profound self-respect, and self-love, which manifest outwardly through enhanced relationships and professional success.

You possess remarkable potential, whether you see it or not. Now is the time to level up, to quiet your impostor syndrome and start leading with your brilliance.

POWER WITHOUT PERMISSION

What Is a Leader?

In this book, we will challenge many traditional definitions—like success, failure, and rejection—and leadership is no exception. It is a thread that weaves through every chapter. So, I don't want you to move forward without first understanding what I mean when I use the word "leader," because it may not match what you've previously been taught or what you think. And we're not here to chase a one-size-fits-all vision of achievement, so let's take a moment to redefine the word "leader."

Being a leader has nothing to do with the title on your email signature or the number of people who report to you. It doesn't require a promotion, a corner office, or a C-suite role. Those things can be part of leadership, but they aren't what define it. The pinnacle of female success is not simply reaching the top of a corporate ladder. For some, a leadership role in an organization may be the dream, and that's beautiful. For others, leadership might look like raising children with intention, showing up with integrity in a support role, or starting a side business rooted in purpose.

So, at its core, leadership is about how you show up in the world, and it begins with how you show up for yourself. How do you make decisions when no one's watching? How do you speak to yourself? How do you move through fear? How do you show up when life gets messy or uncertain? You see, leadership doesn't start when someone hands you a team; it starts when you choose to take responsibility for your own growth, impact, and presence. As you read, I invite you to see yourself as a leader, because that's where your journey can truly begin.

So, to help you navigate your current leadership position—whether you just entered the corporate world, work for a startup, or have your own business—I've created the Leadership Awareness Ladder (LAL). Models may not always be the most accurate, but in this case, I believe having a model is better than having no model at all—because leadership is not a one-size-fits-all, nor is it linear.

Maybe you've heard the saying: "If you've met one child on the autism spectrum, you've met one child on the spectrum." Leadership is similarly abstract and diverse. If you are an outstanding leader in crises, that doesn't automatically mean you're strong in every leadership category.

The Leadership Awareness Ladder

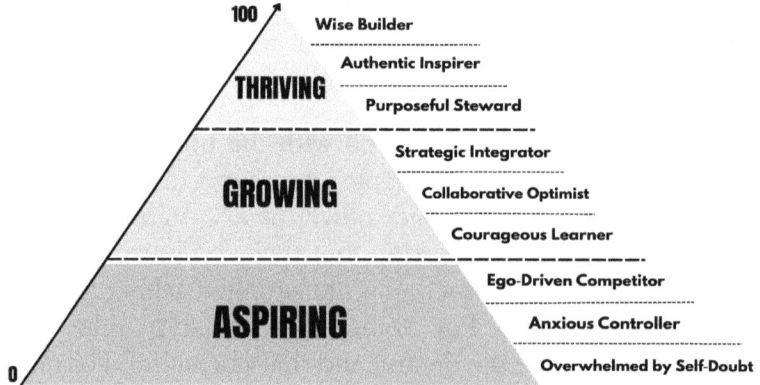

At first glance, this ladder may seem overwhelming, but don't worry—it's simpler than it looks. Let's walk through it together.

Think of this model as a simple ladder made of nine rungs, organized into three zones: Aspiring, Growing, and Thriving.

- The Aspiring Zone reflects reactive, insecure, and ego-driven leadership.
- The Growing Zone reflects steady growth, emotional maturity, and strategic self-awareness.
- The Thriving Zone represents elevated leadership grounded in purpose, impact, and self-mastery.

Each rung aims to represent a typical mindset and a predictable way of showing up—for yourself, your team, and the people you answer to—through five different characteristics: mindset, self-view, team-view, manager-view, and decision habit. (If you don't have a team or a manager, then consider how you relate to people in your life, such as friends, parents, in-laws, etc.)

- Mindset represents your dominant inner stance.
- Self-view represents how you talk to yourself.
- Team-view represents how you see and treat your direct reports, collaborators, friends, and partners.
- Manager-view represents how you relate upward to managers, execs, clients, and investors.
- Decision habit represents what you typically do under pressure.

Notice that next to each ladder rung is a number. This is the Leadership Awareness Score (LAS) that goes from zero to one-hundred. The exact number isn't the point—your direction is. Higher scores signal clearer, values-aligned leadership; lower scores signal patterns you can grow beyond.

The Nine Rungs (Bottom Up)

ASPIRING ZONE

Level 1 – Overwhelmed by Self-Doubt (LAS ~0–10)

- **Mindset:** "I'm not ready."
- **Self-view:** Harsh inner critic, avoids visibility.
- **Team-view:** People feel risky and keep their distance.
- **Manager-view:** Gatekeeper to fear or approval.
- **Decision habit:** Delay, withdraw, or over-control small things.
- **Next move:** Name one fear out loud. Make one small ask today.

Level 2 – Anxious Controller (LAS ~11–21)

- **Mindset:** "If I don't control it, it will fail."
- **Self-view:** Fragile confidence, hyper-vigilant.
- **Team-view:** Micromanages and corrects more than coaches.
- **Manager-view:** Over-prepares to avoid critique and hides risks.

- **Decision habit:** Optimize to avoid blame and don't create value.
- **Next move:** Share context you've been holding. Delegate one small decision fully.

Level 3 – Ego-Driven Competitor (LAS ~22–33)

- **Mindset:** "I must win to be worthy."
- **Self-view:** Confidence tied to comparison.
- **Team-view:** People as tools or rivals. Credit flows up, blame flows down.
- **Manager-view:** Stepstone or obstacle. Respect is transactional.
- **Decision habit:** Choose high-visibility work over high impact.
- **Next move:** Ask for feedback on one behavior. Give public credit to someone else.

GROWING ZONE

Level 4 – Courageous Learner (LAS ~34–35)

- **Mindset:** "I can learn my way through."
- **Self-view:** Work-in-progress. Willing to try and own up to mistakes.
- **Team-view:** Invites input; shares context; experiments.
- **Manager-view:** Brings options with pros/cons. Asks for guidance.
- **Decision habit:** Small, reversible bets. Iterates.
- **Next move:** Run a two-week experiment with clear success criteria.

Level 5 – Collaborative Optimist (LAS ~45–55)

- **Mindset:** "We win together."
- **Self-view:** Secure and humble. Shares credit with others.

- **Team-view:** Assigns by strengths. Balances empathy with standards.
- **Manager-view:** Aligns openly and surfaces trade-offs early.
- **Decision habit:** Includes the right voices and balances speed, quality, and learning.
- **Next move:** Praise one specific strength per person this week.

Level 6 – Strategic Integrator (LAS ~56–66)

- **Mindset:** "Design the system, not just the task."
- **Self-view:** Calm, principled, capable of hard calls.
- **Team-view:** Develops owners and builds repeatable mechanisms.
- **Manager-view:** Proactive partner who uses data and values to decide.
- **Decision habit:** Principled trade-offs across near-, mid-, and long-term.
- **Next move:** Write a one-page roadmap with three bets and kill criteria.

THRIVING ZONE

Level 7 – Purposeful Steward (LAS ~67–77)

- **Mindset:** "Results through people."
- **Self-view:** Steward of the mission. Ego is light and responsibility is high.
- **Team-view:** Humans first; removes blockers; mentors consistently.
- **Manager-view:** Aligns with clarity and signals risks to protect people.
- **Decision habit:** Grow people and results together.
- **Next move:** Create a growth pact with each direct report.

Level 8 – Authentic Inspirer (LAS ~78–89)

- **Mindset:** "Meaning fuels momentum."
- **Self-view:** Integrated and resilient; purpose is clear.
- **Team-view:** Connects day-to-day to a compelling why. Forges alliances.
- **Manager-view:** Enrolls stakeholders with conviction and transparency.
- **Decision habit:** Invests in what scales impact and prunes the rest.
- **Next move:** Start a weekly ritual that spotlights learning and customer value.

Level 9 – Wise Builder (LAS ~90–100)

- **Mindset:** "Do what is right, build what will last."
- **Self-view:** Clear-eyed, grounded, and present.
- **Team-view:** Creates space for others to lead. Codifies culture.
- **Manager/Board-view:** Partners as equals. Anchors debates in values.
- **Decision habit:** Thinks second- and third-order effects. Acts with calm integrity.
- **Next move:** Name your successors. Start transferring authority and know-how.

A Quick Self-Quiz

Check all the statements that feel true most days:

- ☐ Under pressure, I still speak to myself with respect.
- ☐ I set and keep healthy boundaries.
- ☐ I ask for feedback and use it.
- ☐ I make timely decisions with imperfect information.
- ☐ I tell the truth kindly, even when it's hard.
- ☐ I delegate outcomes, not just tasks.
- ☐ My team knows our "why."
- ☐ I coach at least one person each month.

☐ I manage up with clarity and solutions.
☐ I protect thinking time on my calendar.
☐ I celebrate learning, not just results.
☐ I develop leaders who develop others.

If you have zero to four checks, you are in the aspiring zone. If you have five to eight checks, you are in the growing zone. If you have nine to twelve checks, you are in the thriving zone. If you're split, pick the lower zone and use the *Next move* from that zone for 30 days. To figure out which of the nine leadership profiles you have, read the three rungs within your zone and choose the one that currently relates to you the most.

A Final Note

Keep in mind that this ladder is not meant to box you in, make you feel judged, or act as a life sentence. It is merely a tool for reflection and growth on your mindset—and you don't have to live at one rung forever. In fact, you'll probably notice parts of yourself in multiple rungs. That's normal.

My primary objective with this book is to guide you up the leadership ladder. Section II: Awareness will help you navigate the **Aspiring Zone**. Section III: Direction & Action will help you navigate the **Growing Zone**. Last but not least, Section IV: Purpose & Transformation will help you rise into the **Thriving Zone**. So, be sure to do the "next move" within your current zone. Take this quiz again and again. Do the exercises and practices at the end of each chapter. All of this will help you progress toward greater awareness, purpose, and leadership impact.

Speaking of quizzes and exercises, I envision two approaches you might take with this book:

1. Read the entire book first, and return later to complete the activities. While acceptable, this method may delay or dilute your growth. So, at the very least, take a few

minutes after each chapter to reflect on what you've read and learned.
2. Complete the activities as they appear at the end of each chapter before moving on to the next. This method ensures maximum engagement, deeper learning, and tangible progress toward thriving. As you'll notice, I'll be nudging you throughout the book to do it this way.

Either way, this book can only help you if you commit fully, engage with the material, and allow yourself to lead with your brilliance.

Section II: Awareness
See Your Potential in the Rough Stone

Chapter 2: Overcoming Impostor Syndrome

"Even our worst enemies don't talk about us the way we talk to ourselves... I wish someone would invent a tape recorder that we could attach to our brains to record everything we tell ourselves. We would realize how important it is to stop this negative self-talk." — Ariana Huffington

Before we can fully embrace our power and brilliance, we first must see ourselves clearly: who we are, where we are, and the stories we've been telling ourselves. So the most important place to begin is with your current struggle: impostor syndrome and maybe some of its pesky accomplices like perfectionism or insecure overachieving.

Each of these mindsets can be quietly debilitating and, quite frankly, dangerous—because they aren't fleeting thoughts but pervasive internal narratives that make us feel unworthy and undeserving. That's why they can undermine even the most capable individuals and professionals.

In this chapter, we'll explore the root causes of these patterns, how they show up in high-achieving individuals, and, most importantly, how to dismantle them. You'll also hear from my colleague Martha, whose transformation offers both inspiration and a practical blueprint for change.

What Is Impostor Syndrome?

Interestingly, impostor syndrome often affects high performers and the most accomplished individuals—the people you'd least expect. It's characterized by a persistent internal narrative that their success is unearned or fraudulent, and that sooner or later, they'll be "found out." Rather than having a single cause, impostor syndrome typically arises from a combination of factors: early childhood conditioning, societal expectations, low self-worth, trauma, predisposed personality traits, and the distorted realities portrayed on social media (so stop doomscrolling, people!).

While impostor syndrome affects both women and men, it's striking *how* it affects women compared to men. Men with impostor syndrome often *refrain* from success, shying away from feedback and dodging challenges to avoid being exposed. Women, on the other hand, tend to do the opposite. They *pursue* more success—welcoming feedback, powering through challenges, and stretching into new roles—all in an effort to prove their worth (Paulise, 2023).

Ironically, for many women, this pursuit can feel like further proof that they're not qualified. Since no one is instantly excellent at something new, the inner critic keeps repeating: "See? You can't even do this!" But here's the paradox: Who in their right mind would keep chasing things they've never done before and aren't immediately good at? An impostor? No—a woman with grit. A woman with leadership potential.

So, if you find yourself in this loop—always pushing for more, never quite feeling "enough," pause and ask yourself: *What if this isn't evidence that I'm an impostor… but actually evidence that I'm extremely bold?* Because that's the truth. You are bold. You are powerful. You don't need any permission to be brilliant.

The most challenging aspect of impostor syndrome, regardless of gender, is its cyclical nature. Everyone who experiences it hears the same inner critic whisper: "I'm not good enough," "I'm not smart enough," "I don't belong here." Then, they subconsciously seek evidence to support those beliefs—minimizing their successes and magnifying perceived failures. In doing so, they reinforce the false narrative, stifling their growth, eroding their self-esteem and self-worth, and limiting their potential. What's worse, they likely aren't even aware of the pattern because it happens unconsciously. And so, with each success or failure, they repeat, repeat, repeat.

Professionally, impostor syndrome can be paralyzing. It discourages risk-taking and innovation, undermines leadership and executive presence, and fosters a chronic fear of exposure—so those experiencing it don't speak up. Ultimately, this is a disservice to both the individual and the organization because someone is paying them for their time, voice, and opinions. Not only are these employees underutilizing their skills, but they're also wasting energy stuck on a mental hamster wheel—convincing themselves over and over that they are undeserving. Over time, this cycle often leads to burnout, as individuals overextend themselves in an attempt to compensate for their perceived inadequacy.

But impostor syndrome doesn't stop at work. It hurts your personal life too—driving people to overperform and prove themselves to friends, family, and romantic partners. The first step toward overcoming impostor syndrome is recognizing its presence in your life. You can't address what you don't see, so only through acknowledgement can you begin to disarm it.

Similar Faces of Impostor Syndrome

Perfectionism

Perfectionism isn't simply a desire to excel; it's a compulsive need to avoid failure at all costs—in your actions, outcomes, and appearance. It's driven by the belief that anything less than flawless is unacceptable, shaped by things like societal pressures, social media, and growing competition in academic and professional spaces. The result? Chronic dissatisfaction, anxiety, and a constant sense of falling short.

There are several forms of perfectionism:

- **Self-oriented perfectionism** is when individuals impose unattainable standards on themselves.
- **Other-oriented perfectionism** is when those same unrealistic standards are projected onto others—colleagues, employees, or partners.
- **Socially-prescribed perfectionism** stems from the belief that others expect perfection, often leading to anxiety and fear of judgment.

Regardless of the type, each variation inhibits authenticity, collaboration, and well-being—especially in high-stakes professional environments.

Let's take a look at all three forms in action:

- **Self-oriented perfectionism:** Vanessa is the type of manager who triple-checks everything and refuses to miss a day of work, even when she's sick. She often thinks, *"If I don't do this perfectly right, I'm a failure."*
- **Other-oriented perfectionism:** Her perfection doesn't stop with herself. She micromanages her team's work and will even redo their work when she believes it falls short. While reviewing deliverables, she thinks, *"If they can't meet my standards, I'll just do it myself."*
- **Socially-prescribed perfectionism:** Whether it's her own work she's picking on, or someone else's, Vanessa feels a constant, invisible pressure—certain that people are scrutinizing her every move. As she walks toward her office, a thought pops into her mind: *"They're probably thinking I'm not cut out for this job."*

As you can see, the thoughts that accompany perfectionism are daunting. Do you see yourself in Vanessa at all?

Insecure Overachiever Syndrome

Insecure overachievers often present as intelligent, ambitious, and polished. But beneath the surface lies a deep-rooted self-doubt that fuels their relentless pursuit of success. These individuals constantly ask themselves, *"Am I enough?"* and use performance as a means to earn external validation. (That was me.)

While they are achieving on paper, their drive doesn't stem from healthy ambition—it's fueled by fear, not purpose. And fear-driven success is neither sustainable nor satisfying. Because they don't appreciate their own progress, and constantly move the goal post, their accomplishments never feel sufficient enough.

Why does this matter? Because without self-compassion or internal acknowledgment, self-worth can't exist.

Let's put it into a real-world example:

Alice was promoted twice in three years, yet never felt she had actually earned it. She said yes to every project, regularly volunteered to help others, and responded to emails even on her days off. Her schedule was always packed with networking events, strategy sessions, and meetings. To everyone around her, she was unstoppable. But something starkly different was going on for Alice.

The thoughts on loop in her mind sounded like:

- "I can't slow down. If I do, they'll realize I'm not that efficient or successful."
- "I can't say no, or they'll think I'm not dependable."
- "If I don't do everything, I'll be replaced."

As you can see, Alice's success wasn't driven by passion—it was driven by fear. And that kind of drive is not sustainable. (Remember how fear was my driving force too?) Do you see yourself in Alice? (Or me?)

And Even More Faces

If you haven't recognized too much of yourself in any of the descriptions yet, consider if any of these other impostor archetypes sound familiar (Marter, 2023):

- The Soloist: You believe asking for help means weakness, so you insist on doing everything alone.
- The Expert: You feel like a fraud unless you know everything, so you are always chasing another credential, training, or certification.
- The Natural Genius: You believe true ability should come effortlessly, so if something takes effort, you decide you're simply not good enough at it.

- The Super Hero: You measure your worth by how flawlessly you can juggle millions of things without showing signs of fatigue.

Self-Quiz on Impostor Syndrome

Let's pause for a few moments and take a self-evaluation quiz.

Put a check mark next to the statements that feel true for you:

- ☐ I tend to downplay or minimize my achievements.
- ☐ Compliments or praise are uncomfortable for me to accept.
- ☐ I say yes to others even when I'm already stretched thin.
- ☐ Resting or relaxing often makes me feel guilty.
- ☐ I replay conversations in my head, worrying I said the wrong thing.
- ☐ I sometimes fear I don't fully belong in my role.
- ☐ I keep ideas to myself because I'm not sure they're "good enough."
- ☐ I worry I'll be exposed if I don't have an answer for everything.
- ☐ If it doesn't come easily, I question if I am truly capable.
- ☐ I measure my worth by how much I get done.

If you have one to two check marks, then impostor syndrome is not dominating your life. If you have three to five, impostor syndrome is likely a recurring pattern that somewhat affects your life. If you have six or more check marks, then impostor syndrome is an active force shaping your life, likely draining and limiting you. The good news is you're not broken, you're not an impostor—and you are definitely not alone.

Inner Child Work: Reclaiming the Driver's Seat

Here's the reality: You are not your five-year-old self. Nor your teenage self. Nor the version of you who failed, fell apart, or felt rejected five years ago. And yet, those outdated versions of you may still be controlling your present reality.

Let's put it into a metaphor (you know I love these): Imagine navigating rush hour traffic in Manhattan. Would you ever hand the wheel to your seven-year-old self? How about your sixteen-year-old self? Of course not. And yet, many of us allow those early emotional versions of ourselves—terrified, insecure, unhealed, and loud—to be in control. Meanwhile, the adult you is buckled in the backseat, just watching, with no idea where you're headed.

That's where inner child work comes in. It's the process of identifying the moments in your past where core wounds were formed, and offering those younger selves the compassion, encouragement, validation, and safety they didn't receive. By consciously "reparenting" yourself (or working with a therapist), you gradually reclaim control of your life—and your future.

Breaking Free from the Elephant Chains

I've got another metaphor for you: In circuses, baby elephants are tethered to heavy chains, circling a pole in the ground. As they attempt to break free, they fall to the ground, injuring themselves. After enough failed attempts, they stop trying altogether. Years later, even as full-grown, powerful animals, they remain tethered by nothing more than a flimsy decorative rope or collar—because they believe escaping is impossible without immense pain.

Humans experience similar conditioning. From a young age, we are bound by projections, labels, and self-limiting beliefs. Over time, beliefs like "I'm not enough," "I must be perfect," "If I speak up, I'll be abandoned," or "If I speak up, I might get hurt" become mental shackles.

I've seen countless amazingly talented executives drag these unconscious beliefs into boardrooms, leadership roles, and relationships. Even as we age or succeed, those outdated stories can still quietly govern our decisions—holding us back from joy, authenticity, and fulfillment. And so, we remain imprisoned by our own minds.

The good news? You are not a circus elephant. You can break the chains. But first, you have to recognize them for what they are.

Martha's Story: Rewriting the Voice Within

Whether it's impostor syndrome or one of its counterparts, transformation is possible with awareness and effort. I've done it. My colleague Martha has done it. And so can you. Her story is one of pure vulnerability and relatability, and I have no doubt that it will inspire you.

> *"You'll never be good enough to be a VP. You lack the assertiveness to influence your peers. You should have done better."*
>
> *I listened hard to what she was telling me and thought, "She's right, I'm not good enough." All of my failures have one thing in common: me. So I must be the problem.*
>
> *That aggressive feedback wasn't coming from a bad manager—it was coming from a far more menacing bully: my inner saboteur. For as long as I could remember, I'd been in a constant struggle to be the best.*
>
> *My desire to excel was propelled by my family. Neither of my parents finished college—and that was a chip on their shoulders. From a very young age, they emphasized the importance of excelling at school. If I wanted to be successful, I had to achieve academically. They were so adamant about this that we moved to a house that would put us just 0.8 miles within the district for the best local high school, one of the top-ranked schools in Illinois.*
>
> *Once I started writing papers, even in elementary school, it became a rule that my dad had*

to proofread my work before I turned anything in. He was always working and rarely home for dinner, so I'd hop on the family computer, print out my paper, and place it on the nightstand next to his bed. The next morning, I'd find my work marked up in red: This doesn't make sense! You should write this instead. No, no, no! (Even now, my dad occasionally emails me suggestions for improving my LinkedIn posts, which rarely live up to his standards of professionalism.)

My mom was no different. If I got a B+ on a test—which is objectively a great grade—the first thing out of her mouth was, "Why isn't this an A? What happened?" Suffice it to say, if I wasn't at the top of the class, I was doing something wrong.

Then there were my older brothers. They're smart—especially the one closest in age to me. He's something of a genius. He was pulled into a gifted program straight away, maintained a 4.0 GPA, received full-ride academic scholarships to Purdue and Stanford, and was valedictorian at every graduation. He even completed a Master's in Aerospace Engineering at Stanford in just one year instead of two. See? Genius. I'll never forget the look of disappointment on teachers' faces when they realized I wasn't another prodigy. "Spalding smarts," they called it—and apparently, I didn't have them.

Still, I never gave up. I believed that if I just tried harder, studied longer, pushed myself more, I could measure up. In high school, I took Advanced Placement (AP) classes in most subjects and stayed up well past midnight studying. I used to constantly snack on pretzels as a way to keep myself awake, and you wouldn't believe the number of times I woke up with a chewed pretzel in my mouth. Out of a graduating class of 682, I ranked #82. Top 12%.

Looking back, I'm impressed by that. But at the time, I lamented that it wasn't higher. After all, my brother was ranked number one.

The pressure I placed on myself didn't leave room for self-reflection. I was constantly berating myself, then quickly patching over the wounds so I could keep pushing forward. I figured that once I was successful, everything would get better.

I attended the University of Illinois at Urbana-Champaign on an academic scholarship and graduated six months early with honors and a Bachelor's in Journalism. I could have graduated even earlier, but instead chose to take extracurricular courses in the Scandinavian Department. My great-grandparents on my dad's side were from Sweden, so I appreciated the chance to connect with my roots.

That summer, I met Simon—a journalism grad student from Sweden. Instead of attending Northwestern for a Master's in Journalism, I followed my heart and relocated to Sweden to start a life with him. It wasn't the path my parents preferred, but I'm still here 17 years later. I attended Lund University and studied Literature-Culture-Media, one of their Master's programs taught in English.

Even though I was following my heart, I couldn't shake the need to prove myself. The two-year program only required one class per semester. One! But that felt unthinkable to me. My overachieving self simply couldn't allow it. So, I signed up for more classes, despite my counselor warning me she'd never seen a student do that. By the end of my degree, I'd taken 70% more classes than required.

After graduating, I tried to work as a journalist—but I wanted to write in English, not Swedish. In 2010, there weren't many options. I briefly worked remotely for an English-language paper in the country of Georgia, but back then, laptops didn't have webcams. Can you even remember that? I quickly got bored talking with my editor and others through a blank computer screen. It didn't compare to the bustling energy of a newsroom. So, I had to look elsewhere.

Eventually, I landed a full-time job as a Marketing Creative Writer at a security software company based in Copenhagen, Denmark. I was thrilled to get a real job and have an American manager—but also felt like a fraud. I knew nothing about marketing. I'd never done it before. Plus, marketers were the butt of journalism jokes. A saying from J-school rang in my head: "Marketers are just journalists who didn't succeed." Well, I guessed that was me.

To settle into the role, I leaned into my journalism skills. I read everything I could about security and interviewed every product manager I could about their products, industry, and customer base. I simply couldn't settle for not understanding something. That curiosity, which I saw as a weakness, turned out to be a major asset.

Andreas, a product manager at the company, saw my drive for answers as "That woman has potential." As he got to know me, he also saw that I was struggling with self-doubt. One day, he introduced me to the term impostor syndrome and said it sounded like I had it. I had never heard of it before. But after that discussion I spent countless hours researching and reading every article I could find. I was stunned. I'd spent so much of my life with feelings of inadequacy, replaying failures, doubting compliments, brushing off praise, obsessing over flaws—and I thought that was normal. Wasn't everyone second-guessing themselves? Didn't everyone think that if someone said "Great job!" the person was just saying it to be nice and didn't really mean it?

I agreed that I did have impostor syndrome, but having a name for the experience didn't automatically make my unhealthy habits go away. Meanwhile, Andreas continued to push me. There was a new job opening on the VP of Product's team for a Product Marketing Manager. I wanted it, but I didn't think I was qualified (impostor syndrome!).

Through Andreas' encouragement, I called the VP. And I'll never forget that phone call. I was so anxious. The first thing out of my mouth was, "Hi, so I hear there's an opening on your team, and I'd like to express my interest in the position." She chuckled and said, "OK, and how are you doing, Martha?" I almost died on the other end! I was so desperate to achieve that I'd completely neglected basic human interaction skills. Despite my embarrassing opening, I got the job and did it well. In fact, I did it so well that, over time, I became the sole product marketer for our new hardware line. I loved the team, and, most days, I honestly looked forward to going to work.

But then came the one constant that always rears its head: change. The company went through a reorganization. The VP of Product left. New leadership came in. It didn't take long for me to realize I was no longer happy there; I didn't share the same values as the new management, and I needed to move on after almost seven years.

After sending out just a couple of applications, I landed my next opportunity: I would be the only product marketing manager at a language management company. That meant I'd have to define what success looked like and create processes from scratch. I seriously considered telling my new manager that hiring me was a mistake and I couldn't do it (more impostor syndrome!), but my desire to succeed stopped me. I liked my manager and the team, but after a year-and-a-half–change. My manager and several colleagues left. I was reporting directly to the CEO, and, again, I reached a point where I was no longer happy. I wondered if I was the problem—if my unhappiness was a sign I wasn't performing well enough (even more impostor syndrome!).

Nonetheless, I needed a new position. I heard through my network about an opening at a cybersecurity company. My gut reaction told me no, but I figured a coffee meeting to learn more wouldn't hurt.

I met a senior leader from the company at a small coffee shop near their office in Copenhagen. I had a paper copy of my CV in my bag and had been practicing typical interview questions. That "coffee meeting" turned into an interview—but instead of asking me to defend my abilities, he spent the full hour and a half trying to convince me that the company was the right fit for me. It totally threw me. I had another, more formal, interview at the office five days later, and then accepted the job as Head of Product Marketing.

Years later, I asked him about that coffee meeting, and how he knew I could do the job. It turns out my previous manager had told him, "As long as you keep Martha interested in the role, you'll have a loyal and hard-working employee. Hiring her will be the best decision you ever make." I had no idea the impression I'd made on her. It floored me. I thought I was just doing my job—what was so special about that? I quickly brushed aside the tremendous praise of my abilities as nothing more than her being nice (impostor syndrome, yet again!).

That job was intense in all the best ways. In the nearly five years I was there, I pushed myself to develop skills I never thought I was capable of. I built up product marketing as a discipline and created processes. I hired employees for the first time and built a team. I was awarded Employee of the Year after my first year. I learned how to be a leader. I was promoted to lead the full marketing team as Marketing Director. I transformed the marketing team from a group of demotivated people into a collaborative, highly satisfied team. Best of all, among these achievements, I finally took the necessary steps to face and start to conquer my impostor syndrome.

At some point, my manager realized that my lack of belief in myself and my abilities wasn't going to just go away. He truly cared about me and my development (which sounds simple, yet it's shocking how many leaders fail at this), so he suggested I see a leadership coach. I'd had mentors before, but this was different. This was someone whose sole job was to help me grow. My coach never made me feel unqualified. She never questioned my abilities. She created the psychological safety I needed to talk about anything. She didn't hand me the answers, but she gave me the confidence and support to uncover them myself.

In one of our sessions, she made a statement that caught me off guard: "Martha, you are very hard on yourself. You're trying to be the best parts of all these people and beating yourself up when you don't meet superhero levels. You're ignoring everything that's going well." I was dumbfounded. Until that point in my career, I had always focused on what was going wrong—constantly optimizing the last few percentage points instead of reveling in the overwhelming majority of success I had created. Celebrating others' success but ignoring my own. Tearing myself down over failures, but exonerating others from theirs.

And because of these bad habits, I was always talking to myself in terrible ways. That's when my coach suggested the most difficult, yet most helpful exercise I've ever done to combat my impostor syndrome: I would sit on one side of the table as my "mean" self and speak out loud my worst thoughts about myself. Then I would move to the other side of the table and tell my "mean" self how those words made me feel.

Afterward, I couldn't stop crying. The undeserved vitriol I spoke about myself was shocking. Hearing myself say such hateful things opened my eyes to how serious the problem really was. How could I ever succeed as a leader, a mom, or even a person if this was how I thought about myself? I wouldn't say those kinds of things about people I didn't even respect—so why was I saying them to myself?

The exercise was a turning point. Because if I instead spent that time and energy building myself up, it felt like there would be no limits to what I could achieve. My team consistently had the highest scores in employee surveys because I was a good leader—not because they were just being nice. I deserved Employee of the Year because I delivered amazing work—not because management was just trying to build my confidence. The positive feedback people gave me was sincere, not just something people say. It wasn't overnight, but through working with my coach, I gained the confidence to squash my feelings of inferiority.

Another practical tool that helped me was keeping track of all the positive feedback I received. I have a folder on my computer where I've saved encouraging emails and notes from coworkers, dating back to my first job in Sweden. If I feel the negative self-talk coming, I pull out those notes and remind myself of what others have said. It helps keep "mean Martha" at bay and reignites my positive mindset.

I will always cherish my time at the cybersecurity company—and my coworkers—for how much I grew during those years. But just like all my other jobs, eventually, change came. The company was acquired by a private equity firm, and almost the entire management team left, including the CEO. I didn't share the same values as the new management, and this time, I was confident enough in my abilities to recognize that. So when I was offered a new position at the company, I said no. Many people were shocked—and sad. But I knew it was time to continue growing somewhere else.

As I took time to consider my next career move, impostor syndrome smacked me in the face again—this time through the older of my two sons. Both my boys play basketball and are among the top players on their teams. They regularly do drills outside of practice, and with my husband's background as a competitive diver at an elite level, he helps them train effectively.

When my oldest son feels he's not performing well, he can be pretty hard on himself. At first, I thought, "But isn't everyone like that with sports?" But then, during one tough game, he had a nasty fall and said he couldn't play the rest of the game because he'd sprained his ankle. Later, his ankle healed surprisingly fast. He couldn't quite articulate it, but when we talked, it sounded like he had overemphasized the pain because he was worried about losing the game for his team.

Alarm bells went off in my head. The same thing was happening at school. He typically scores 100% on his exams, and when he doesn't perform perfectly, he's hard on himself. While I knew we needed to keep an eye on him, I hadn't realized how much this mindset was affecting his daily life. I talked with my husband, and we made a point to start giving our boys more thoughtful feedback—not just "Good job," but specifically highlighting where they were excelling. We hoped this would help them see the value they brought to their respective teams and recognize their successes in school.

I thought things were turning around—until one Sunday morning, when my oldest son wanted to bake cookies. He'd helped me a lot when he was younger but had never baked on his own. I pulled out a recipe and stayed right next to him in case he had questions.

He was doing great—measuring everything carefully and following each step closely. But when it came time to crack the eggs, which he had never done before, a bit of eggshell landed in the batter. Immediately, he hit his head and said, "I'm so stupid. I will never be good at this."

My heart dropped to the floor. At that moment, I realized he was suffering from the same feelings of impostor syndrome. It wasn't enough to just be a supportive mom—I had to give him the tools to recognize it and manage it. I used one of the techniques my coach had used with me. "Hey, think about your friend Olle. He's never cracked an egg before. If he did it for the first time and a bit of shell fell into the batter, would you think he's stupid?" He looked up at me and shook his head. "Then why do you think you're stupid?" Sometimes, simple questions lead to major revelations.

If I let impostor syndrome win me over, it would likely win over my kids too. That experience with my sons gave me even more motivation to keep believing in my abilities and to speak to myself with compassion. I get to be an example for them, and even more than I want a successful career, I want to be a successful mom.

As for my next career move, I teamed up with two former colleagues, and we started our own company. It was a huge leap for me, and honestly, I don't think I would have had the confidence to do it if I hadn't been doing this work on myself. Sure, some days that little voice still whispers, "This will never work." But now? I have the tools to shut it down.

I don't think I'll ever be completely "over" impostor syndrome. But I've learned how to recognize it, manage it, and keep it from running my thoughts—and that's vital for leadership. It's not about never having doubts; it's about not letting those doubts stop you. It's about confidence, not perfection. And for me, it's about showing my sons that being kind to yourself is a strength—not a weakness.

Just recently, my older son decided that he wants to attend a middle school that specializes in basketball. To get in, he needs to try out and be selected. The other day, we biked past the school, and he said, "I'll go here if I make it in... No, wait... when I make it in." I smiled. It was a small shift, but a win in the battle to manage his thoughts.

So if, while you've been reading this, you were thinking, "This sounds like me,"—know that you're not alone. Consider working with a coach.

Save positive feedback and compliments. Push back on that negative voice in your head. You don't need to be perfect to achieve—you just need to believe that you belong. And you do.

Martha exemplifies what's possible when we shift from external approval to internal grounding. When I first introduced her to the concept of impostor syndrome, it simply planted a seed. The real work—getting curious, doing the research, and confronting her fears—was entirely her own. That's the most important takeaway: This work is deeply personal. No one can do it for you. However, I promise it's entirely achievable, and you will also stop perpetuating generational pain in the process.

The Importance of Self-Validation

Here's the truth: You are remarkable. You have overcome challenges, acquired expertise, and demonstrated resilience. You have skills and qualities that make you uniquely capable. Now, we need you to believe that for yourself, because what differentiates thriving professionals from everyone else doesn't merely come down to skillset; it comes down to who can validate themselves internally.

External validation can be fleeting and conditional, and can lead to feelings of emptiness and anxiousness. Self-validation, by contrast, can be strong and unwavering, and lead to peace and stability. It involves accepting and affirming your worth, regardless of outcomes, titles, or accolades. And when you practice self-validation, you build confidence and resilience in the face of adversity and criticism.

So, how do you cultivate self-validation? By developing a better relationship with yourself:

- Celebrate your achievements—no matter how small.
- Speak to yourself with compassion, especially in moments of difficulty.
- Stop obsessing over others' and their credentials.

- Appreciate the fact that you're taking action—that's progress.
- Set realistic, sustainable goals.
- See failure as *data*, not as a *verdict*.
- Instead of comparing yourself to others, compare yourself to the person you were yesterday. (And stop comparing yourself to the person you were ten years ago or the "perfect" people you see across social media.)

The goal isn't to eliminate self-doubt, but to ensure it no longer takes hold of the steering wheel.

As I shared, I've personally walked this path myself. Even after scaling and successfully exiting a business, I found myself battling the same painful internal dialogue: "You're not good enough." That voice won't simply disappear overnight, but if you begin to question it, challenge it, and reframe it, then it will lose its power over you.

Activities for Overcoming Impostor Syndrome

By focusing on self-compassion, embracing imperfections, and building inner confidence, we free ourselves from impostor syndrome. True transformation won't happen just from shifting your mindset, though—it comes from taking action. Below are exercises designed to help you shift from self-doubt to self-assurance. Try at least two of them. (Don't worry, these aren't the only activities. As you read, you will come across a plethora that will help you.)

#1: Reflect on your past:

Journal about moments when you've felt like an impostor. What triggered those feelings? Are there specific memories or experiences that shaped your self-perception?

#2: Try Martha's Exercise:

As you read in Martha's powerful story, set up two chairs in a room. Sit in one and become your "mean" self—saying all the worst, most critical things you believe about yourself. Then, move to the other chair. Reflect on everything the mean version of you just said. How did those harsh words make you feel? Speak your response out loud to the "mean" self. Finally, ask yourself: Is this really the mindset I want to continue operating from?

#3: Track Your Negative Self-Talk:

For one week, tally every negative thought you make about yourself. At the end of each day, review the total. Over time, aim to reduce these tallies. This simple practice cultivates mindfulness, disrupts harmful thought patterns, and helps rewire your neural pathways.

#4: Create a Wall of Affirmations:

Each time someone offers praise or acknowledgment, write it on a sticky note and post it where you'll see it daily (e.g., your bathroom mirror). Over time, you'll create a visual testament to your impact and capabilities. You might also find a recurring theme, which can highlight a specific strength you have but may not have been aware of before. I still do this activity to this day—though now, instead of a wall, I save my praise in a photo album on my phone.

#5: The Power of *Yet*:

Don't get discouraged by what you haven't been able to conquer, accomplish, or master yet. A growth journey is ongoing. Hence, the power of the word yet. This is a great word to start implementing into your vocabulary. "I haven't learned how to do that… yet." "I am not a master at sales… yet." "I haven't gotten the promotion… yet." Keep going!

Call to Action for Leaders

Leaders and CEOs play a critical role in supporting employees who may struggle with Impostor syndrome or perfectionism. Addressing these challenges not only benefits the individual employee but also fosters a healthier work culture and leads to better company results. Make sure that you are doing the following.

#1: Normalize Imperfection:

Create a culture where experimentation is allowed and where challenges, mistakes, and failures are simply seen as part of the process. Model this behavior by experimenting yourself and sharing your learning moments. Most importantly, when your employees experiment and make a mistake, don't blame them. Celebrate their boldness.

#2: Reframe Success Metrics:

Yes, results matter, but they aren't the only thing you should care about. Success is progress over perfection. Success is small wins. Success is when your growth inspires others' growth. Growing people create growing organizations—and the opposite is also true—so shift the success narrative.

#3: Intentionally Recognize Contributions:

High performers often feel invisible. Offer both private and public acknowledgment of their work. When giving feedback, pair areas of improvement with sincere appreciation to foster trust and growth simultaneously.

#4: Teach People How to Say *Thank You*:

Those with impostor syndrome will rarely say "Thank you" when given a compliment. Rather, they ignore it, deflect it, or squirm uncomfortably when receiving one. The next time you notice someone deflecting a compliment, spend a few minutes with them to explain the importance of accepting it, and nudge them to say "Thank you" out loud.

#5: Always State Your Why:

Your employees, in a way, are like your children. You are leading them, and you want to make sure they understand why you are leading them in any given direction. Instead of saying "No!" or "Good job!" without an explanation, explain your *why* behind every decision, statement, or piece of feedback. This way, they won't make assumptions that might be tied to their impostor syndrome, perfectionism, or insecure overachiever tendencies. (Practice this on your children as well. You're welcome!)

A Final Note on Growth Work

A book can only be so long. Thus, I had to do one of the hardest things: cut out material that is valuable, material that you should have access to. But fear not—it can all be found at the QR code below. In addition to any resources mentioned in this chapter, you will find my *Power Without Permission* community which has mini courses, videos, mentors (including myself), guest speakers, and countless tools to help you with impostor syndrome and the other topics in this book. The best part: as I continue my journey with Leaders ADAPT, I will keep adding additional resources into the community that are related to *Power Without Permission* for free.

If you purchased this book, it's completely free for you to join the community.

Just scan this QR code to get started.

Chapter 3: Cultivating Self-Awareness

"The unexamined life is not worth living." — Socrates

If you can see yourself in the patterns of impostor syndrome, then congratulations! You already have some measure of self-awareness. Recognizing the ways you doubt yourself, discount your accomplishments, or undermine your success is the first step toward understanding your inner world.

Now, imagine trying to navigate a foreign city without a GPS, map, or tour guide. You'd likely wander aimlessly and feel completely disoriented. That's precisely what life looks like without self-awareness: directionless, reactive, and riddled with unnecessary detours. (Hint: If your honest answer to the question "Why do you do what you do every day?" is "I don't know," then this chapter is speaking directly to you.)

Self-awareness is the indispensable foundation of any meaningful personal or professional growth journey. It's the conscious understanding of who you are, where you stand, and how you arrived at this point.

Here's the hard truth though: The gateway to self-awareness is personal suffering. Most people aren't truly ready to explore their inner world until they've endured pain—whether it's heartbreak, grief, failure, or disappointment. These experiences often mark our personal "rock bottom," the point at which we begin seeking change and transformation.

The paradox? The deeper and earlier you struggle, the better off you may be—because you'll more quickly come to recognize that your long-held coping mechanisms, many of which were shaped in childhood, are not effective or sustainable in adulthood.

Perhaps you picked up this book because you already hit that bottom. Or maybe these pages will help accelerate that pivotal moment of reckoning, so you can finally stop circling the same patterns. Either way, this chapter will guide you through the principles of self-awareness, the role of identity evolution, and the transformative practice of inner child work. Along the way, you'll hear a powerful and introspective story from my colleague Julie—an example of what genuine self-awareness looks like and why it matters so much.

What Is Self-Awareness?

At its core, self-awareness is the ability to reflect honestly and deeply on your internal landscape. It involves cultivating genuine curiosity about your thoughts, emotions, behaviours, and belief systems. Think of it as developing a strong, supportive relationship with yourself—asking tough questions, listening closely to your feelings, and thoughtfully analysing your triggers and patterns.

Why does it matter? Because self-awareness affects nearly every dimension of our lives. When developed, it enhances decision-making, strengthens confidence, deepens relationships, builds empathy, and amplifies both emotional intelligence and genuine connection.

Despite its significance, most people dramatically overestimate their level of self-awareness. According to psychologist Dr. Tasha Eurich (2018), while 95% of individuals believe they're self-aware, only 10-15% actually are. This stark gap has serious consequences—especially for those in leadership roles. It's an internal misalignment that can lead to defensiveness, blind spots, and professional plateaus.

So, even if you *think* you are among the 10-15% who are truly self-aware, don't assume it with complete certainty. And even if you are in that small group, there's always room to go deeper. Self-awareness is a practice, not a destination, so keep striving for more.

Eurich's research, which involved over 5,000 participants across four years, doesn't stop there. Eurich et al. (2018) identified two primary dimensions of self-awareness: internal and external. Internal self-awareness refers to our ability to understand our values, aspirations, reactions, and impact on others. External self-awareness refers to how accurately we perceive the way others see us.

From these two axes emerge four distinct self-awareness profiles:

- **Seekers:** Individuals low in both internal and external self-awareness. They often feel stuck, disengaged, and disconnected from themselves and others.
- **Pleasers:** High in external but low in internal self-awareness. They're acutely aware of how others perceive them but may lack a strong sense of personal values or boundaries.
- **Introspectors:** High in internal but low in external self-awareness. They know themselves well but resist feedback, fail to challenge their blind spots, and often remain unaware of how others perceive them.
- **Aware:** High in both internal and external self-awareness. These individuals have clarity about who they are and how they show up in the world. They are introspective, open to feedback, and intentional in their growth.

Based on these descriptions, which of these categories do you want to fall into by the time you reach the end of this book? Understanding this is important not only for your personal growth but for professional development as well. Eurich's findings reinforce that the most effective, promotable, trusted, and respected people possess high levels of both internal and external self-awareness.

But insight alone won't bring about transformation—awareness without action is simply intellectual entertainment. So how do we translate this insight into meaningful change? One of the most profound ways is through inner child work.

ANDREAS PETTERSSON

Julie's Story: The Power of Knowing Yourself

I've experienced the power of self-awareness firsthand—in both my own life and in the lives of others, like my colleague Julie. From an early age, she had a remarkable ability to tune inward, reflect, and make conscious choices. That inner clarity became her compass through motherhood, business, and the kinds of life-defining moments that shape us. No matter the circumstance, she has consistently found her way forward with intention and grace—often creating success in ways others might overlook. Her story shows how self-awareness can be one of the greatest assets we carry.

The crazy part is, I've done some of my best work while walking through the darkest, hardest moments of my life. And I'm not saying I simply weathered the storm, waiting for things to get better—I paused and asked myself, "Who am I in this moment, even when everything around me is falling apart?" That pause is what changes everything. It helped me to pull off things most wouldn't have thought possible, right in the middle of the chaos. And if I'm being honest, I'm still finding my way through it.

The truth is, I've been incredibly blessed. For much of my life, I never knew fear, never felt truly alone, never had to worry much about what came next. But life eventually tested me in ways I never expected. When all of these "firsts" came crashing in at once, what carried me through wasn't luck—it was my refusal to let circumstances define my future. It was my self-awareness, my alignment, my unwillingness to accept any version of reality that didn't reflect who I knew I was.

Though to fully understand me and my story, it's best if I take you back a little earlier...

My early life was shaped by unique circumstances, surrounded by passion, success, intelligence, and drive. My family was often in the company of high-achieving individuals, and I truly value that I had a seat at that table—from lunch with the President to late-night strategy talks over dinner.

Among the most important high achievers in my life were my parents. I was at the intersection of two incredible legacies: my mother and my father. My mother, in addition to her many academic and professional accomplishments, had an unwavering devotion to nurturing and mentoring . Her proudest role was being a mom, and she was all-in every single day, making sure my sister and I felt seen, heard, and supported in everything we set our minds to. My father mirrored that same devotion—only his was to service, leadership, and lifelong learning. A Marine General turned Silicon Valley entrepreneur, he earned multiple degrees and fulfilled his dream of moving our family to Northern California, where our family ranch still remains.

My parents shaped my earliest understanding of what it means to live and lead life with heart and conviction. Their influence also revealed two important insights that became foundational to my self-awareness. First, I learned not to idolize anyone for status or fame. I instinctively treated everyone the same, which helped me stay grounded in who I was. Second, I became attuned to how every person impacts a system. From janitors to CEOs, every person matters and every role holds equal value—and that awareness made me deeply conscious of myself and others in group dynamics.

At the same time, because I grew up around such natural, accomplished leaders, I often gravitated toward supporting roles—not because I lacked ambition, but because I unconsciously believed the spotlight belonged to others. That realization took time and self-awareness to uncover. I didn't question it when I first entered the working world at 19.

While still in college, I began working for a startup as a saleswoman. It was as entry-level as sales gets. My job was to cold-call all day with one goal: land a second meeting. I quickly discovered my personality fit the role perfectly. That first month, I became the top salesperson and was named Rookie of the Month. I even closed the company's first major—and largest—deal with eBay. My success was thanks to my self-awareness: I could get people to stay on the phone and engage, and I instinctively knew how to read customers and adjust my approach depending on who I was speaking with. (Awareness of others is just as important as awareness of self!)

Then, life changed in an instant. Just as my career and education were taking off, I found out I was pregnant. At that moment, I knew exactly where I was meant to be. Without hesitation, I stepped away from school and work to embrace a far more important role I had dreamed of for as long as I could remember. I got married at 21, settled at the ranch, and stepped fully into motherhood. I raised four beautiful children, homeschooled them through much of their early years, and fully embraced the gift that it was. Being a mother has been my greatest calling, and I remain grateful for every second of it, now carrying that same gratitude as a grandmother.

What I didn't expect was how much motherhood would teach me about myself. You enter that space thinking you're there to teach your children—and you do—but they also become some of your greatest teachers. Through them, my self-awareness deepened even further. I was constantly faced with who I was: my reactions, my triggers, my tone, my patience, my strengths. Every day was a lesson in pausing, reflecting, and choosing my responses with intention.

By the time my children grew more independent, I felt that pull to step back into the professional world. I joined yet another startup, as employee number three, and was given the flexibility I needed to still prioritize my children. I knew almost instantly it was the right fit. I was back in my element—closing founder-level sales, leading major deals, and reigniting a part of myself I hadn't fully tapped into yet.

That reentry sparked the next chapter of my career in the security industry, where I've now spent over fifteen years. I've worked across every side of it— manufacturing, distribution, integration—but it's never been the work itself that's kept me here. What drives me is creating spaces where people feel safe enough to thrive.

The true turning point in my career came when I joined Andreas' company, though. From our first conversations, I sensed this wouldn't be "just another job." I knew in my gut it was next-level. Soon after I was hired, I traveled to headquarters in Irvine and met Andreas in person over dinner. Later that evening, someone pulled me aside and said, "He really likes you." When I asked why, they shared: "After you left, he said, 'That woman is a natural leader. She should be in management.'"

At the time, I couldn't fully see that for myself— not because the qualities weren't there or because I didn't believe I was capable, but because I'd never considered professional leadership as my path. I respected it deeply but saw it as something other people did, not necessarily me. The irony? I'd been leading my whole life. In school and amongst peers, I naturally led groups. As a mother, I led our household. People have always been drawn to me, turning to me when decisions need to be made or direction set. But I'd never been in a professional environment that called those innate abilities forward.

So, while Andreas didn't create those leadership qualities, he recognized them and created space for them to emerge in a professional context. One day, he said something that really caused me to stop and evaluate: "You're great at what you do, but I believe you could be exceptional in areas you haven't even explored yet. You have strengths you might not even be fully aware of."

That comment made me pause. Until that point, I hadn't questioned leaving sales. I was good at it, I enjoyed it, and I was thriving. But he asked me to take a personality assessment. I didn't score highly in what are typically seen as "traditional sales traits," but I scored off the charts in empathy, emotional intelligence, and customer connection—the very qualities that had fueled my success all along.

That moment shifted everything. I realized my natural wiring wasn't just a personal trait—it was a professional superpower. Andreas offered me a new role built around my natural strengths. I accepted it and became the Director of Customer Experience.

For the first time, I was doing work that wasn't just about skill—it was about who I am. But stepping into leadership also required deeper self-awareness. I had to confront deeply ingrained internal narratives. One time, Andreas asked, "You have such great ideas one-on-one. Why aren't you sharing them in the room?" I told him I didn't think it was my place. He replied, "It is your place. And as a leader, it's your job." Those words challenged something in me. He helped me gain confidence and truly see myself. And as I stepped forward, people responded—they leaned on me, looked to me for input and support, and relied on me in new ways

While my professional life was taking shape in new ways, behind the scenes, everything else was changing. Over the span of a few years, so much in my personal life shifted—divorce, a move to a new state far from close friends and family, and the loss of the home, property, hobbies, and routines I once cherished. My role as a mother changed too. My kids grew up and moved out, leaving behind a quieter house. I also found the greatest love of my life—and, after an unexpected turn, we parted ways.

It was my personal perfect storm.

Loss on its own is hard, but when it comes from every direction at once, it leaves you completely untethered. Everything that once gave my life structure had vanished. But it wasn't just structure I lost— it was everything that brought me joy. No more horses to care for, no property to tend, no trail rides, which had always been my great passion and escape. The constant rhythm of keeping a home alive for my family, all the energy and familiar noise—gone. But perhaps most devastating was losing my greatest love and best friend, and with him, our daily conversations, our shared laughter, all the plans we'd made together.

And what made that period even harder was the emptiness. There was no one to sit with me, no one to distract me, not even hobbies left to redirect my energy. It was just me—sitting in the silence, feeling every bit of it. At times, the weight was so heavy, it would tip toward fear, and if I wasn't careful, it could easily spiral into panic. But the fear itself forced me into reflection—sometimes right in the middle of it—forcing me to dig deep, to interrupt the momentum building inside my own mind before it overtook me.

All those things I once said I never knew—fear, loneliness, worry for my future—I now knew them fully. All at once. I was afraid. I was alone. And I had no idea what would come next.

Through a lot of reflection, I finally started identifying what I was truly up against: heartbreak, loneliness, and boredom. While I couldn't change what had been lost, I could start building toward what I needed. I asked myself again and again: "What are you feeling right now? Why? What can solve it?" That became my starting point. Because true self-awareness isn't about knowing yourself on the surface—it's about pausing long enough to notice what you're feeling, naming it honestly, and then deciding what to do with it.

I began making lists—of hobbies I could try, places I wanted to visit, and ways to meet new people. I signed up to volunteer at the hospital, helping care for premature babies who need lots of touching and holding. I tried yoga, joined a gym, and signed up for pilates—not necessarily for my physical health, but to create even small windows of human interaction where new friendships might form. I committed to at least one daily walk with my dog, no matter the weather or how I felt.

These actions didn't solve everything overnight, but they became stepping stones—small habits that gave me practice in finding simple wins, even in being alone. Some worked. Some didn't. But with every effort I noticed what gave me energy and what drained me, and that's self-awareness in action.

One of the most unexpected wins came on a day I almost skipped my daily walk. While out, I met someone with the same kind of dog. That simple encounter sparked an idea. That night, I created the CDA Bernese Mountain Dog Club (@cda_berners on Instagram), a space for people who shared a common love for the breed. Within weeks, we were hosting playdates, forming friendships, and planning charity events to build community.

Another unexpected gift that helped me was my job. On days when life felt heavy, my job was something I could look forward to—something that energized me, fulfilled me, and challenged me. All because I was willing to step into new roles and take professional leaps.

Today, I truly love what I do. I serve as Director of Human Experience, where my mission is to operationalize empathy and embed human understanding into every part of our company. My role allows me to foster a culture that not only exceeds customer expectations, but also drives internal collaboration to create meaningful, human-centered experiences for both our employees and our customers. Recently, I was offered the opportunity to lead an extraordinary team of UX researchers, and every single one of them is a remarkable woman. In many ways, it feels like the full-circle moment I didn't even realize I was building toward.

Years ago, when Andreas first began mentoring me, he asked for just one thing: "Someday, find a way to mentor at least five women in return." Without hesitation, I promised I would. And now, that promise lives in the very work I do every single day.

This isn't to say my journey is finished or that I've figured everything out. As a leader, a woman, and a human being, I know I'm still evolving, and that's exactly how it should be. After all, self-awareness is not a destination you reach but a practice you commit to. It is the light we carry into the darkest corners of our minds.

> *Some of us are born with a knack for self-awareness, and some of us aren't. Either way, it often won't be deepened in the easy seasons of life. It'll deepen in the sacred messiness. Because that's where we make the most critical choice: to evolve instead of stagnate. To rise instead of retreat. To admit that we can redefine ourselves at any moment—beyond any role, any title, and even our own expectations.*

Yes, Julie began life with certain privileges, but privilege alone does not guarantee courage, clarity, or self-awareness. We all choose how to use what we've been given, and Julie has always chosen to turn her opportunities and awareness into action. Her story reminds us that self-awareness is closely linked to how we relate to fear. While many instinctively run from fear, Julie leans in, transforming it into a catalyst for growth. Think of her message the next time life throws you multiple challenges at once. And just like Julie, ask yourself, "What am I feeling? Where do I go from here?"

A Note About These Guest Stories

Also, just to be clear: I didn't invite these co-authors into this book to praise me. I invited each person to share their insights on topics they've lived through and grown from. I know you've read compliments about me from both of the two stories that have appeared so far, and you will continue to see that throughout this book. I'll be honest and share that when I initially read each story and saw the kind things said about me, I felt awkward. I wondered, "Will readers think I asked for this? Will it come across as self-serving?" I almost decided to delete any mention of me, but then realized why everyone's words needed to stay.

In addition to the fact that it keeps each story raw, authentic, and unchanged, I decided to keep all mentions of me because these women's words highlight something deeply important: I'm not just talking about supporting women or building networks—I'm actually doing it. These women are all part of my real, nontransactional circle. Their stories reflect genuine relationships, not curated endorsements. And, through this process, several core themes we'll discuss in later chapters are naturally being reinforced: overcoming the fear of judgment, building your strategic network, and empowering the next generation of female leaders. So their statements are part of the proof that what you're reading here isn't just theory, but lived experience. Finally, and perhaps most importantly, what these women are reflecting is something you should pay attention to: *Your influence may be bigger than you think, so don't underestimate the power of your words.* For all of these reasons, I couldn't remove these reflections. Not only would that be silencing the truth, but silencing the fact that this kind of leadership—rooted in authenticity, integrity, and purpose—is possible in the first place.

Activities for Cultivating Self-Awareness

After nearly one and a half decades in leadership and personal development, I can say with confidence: Self-awareness is not a soft skill. It's a strategic advantage and cornerstone to powerful leadership. It's not just about introspection—it's about awakening to the truth of who you are, who you've been, and who you are becoming.

If there's one promise I can make in this book, it's this: If you learn to consciously manage your thoughts, behaviors, and beliefs through self-awareness, you will change your life for the better.

So, no more asking yourself, "Where do I start?" You start right here—with yourself. This chapter is both your mirror and your map—a mirror to reflect who you've been, and a map to guide who you're ready to become. Try at least two of the following activities (one of which being the first one). I've personally done all of them and mentored many others through them—and I promise they work. If you feel called to do all five, that's perfectly fine too.

#1: Begin a Journaling Practice

Each day for one week, reflect on one of the following prompts:

- What patterns do I notice in my relationships?
- What beliefs about myself are limiting me?
- When do I feel most alive?
- What are my greatest strengths and weaknesses? (Consider taking the Clifton Strengths assessment to find out—link available via the QR code at the end of this chapter.)
- What illusions do I still cling to?
- When am I at my best—and when am I at my worst?
- How do I recognize and manage fear, anxiety, and frustrations? Why do I feel a certain way about them or respond a certain way to them?

#2: Change Your Phone Habits

Avoid starting and ending your day in passive scrolling mode on social media because it will build an impossible image in your mind about your life and what it "should" be. Instead, replace the first and last 30 minutes of your day with intentional reflection, journaling, or growth-oriented content. Begin and end your day with alignment and purpose—not distraction.

#3: Revisit a Pivotal Childhood Memory

Identify a moment from your past when you formed a limiting belief. What actually happened? Who was involved? Were they angry, misinformed, or projecting their own pain? Could the opposite of that limiting belief also be true? Can you think of other moments that prove the limiting belief wrong? View the memory through adult eyes, and reframe it with compassion. Write a message to that younger version of you, telling them who you are and reminding them that they will be fine.

#4: Work With a Therapist

You don't have to walk this path alone. Therapy can accelerate healing, uncover blind spots, and support deep inner transformation.

#5: Get an Accountability Partner

Growth doesn't have to be a solo mission. Find a mentor, sponsor, colleague, trusted friend, or a community. Sharing your goals—or walking alongside someone on a similar path—can be just what you need to turn intentions into actions.

Call to Action for Leaders

The organizational impact of self-aware employees cannot be overstated. Higher productivity, stronger collaboration, clearer communication, and a more engaged culture all stem from this foundational skill. As a leader, it's your responsibility to set the tone. Start by committing to the following practices:

#1: Implement 360-Degree Feedback

Encourage feedback from peers, managers, and direct reports on each employee's skills, behavior, and performance. This comprehensive approach reveals blind spots that traditional evaluations often miss. Coach and lead your direct reports through the self-awareness process if you are in the thriving zone on the Leadership Awareness Ladder.

#2: Invest in EQ Training

Emotional intelligence workshops benefit your organization on several levels. On an individual and personal level, they help employees develop self-awareness and empathy. Interpersonally, they enhance team communication and resilience. And they help the organization as a whole gain a competitive advantage.

#3: Foster a Culture of Psychological Safety

Create an environment for your team or employees where realness is welcome and imperfection isn't punished. Share your own challenges and wins. Celebrate mistakes as learning opportunities. Encourage honest feedback and reward self-reflection. These practices build trust and psychological safety.

#4: Anchor in the Company's Core Values

Just as you and your employees should know your individual core values (an activity you'll find in Chapter 4: Developing Emotional Intelligence), you need to know and embody the core values of your organization. What are your company's core values? Are they actively guiding decisions and behavior—or just posted on a wall? Which core value will help your employees evolve from being seekers, pleasers, and introspectors to being aware?

#5: Reflect on Your Own Self-Awareness

If you want self-aware employees, you must lead by example. If you are ready to level up as a leader, consider taking a leadership course or self-development training to deepen your own self-awareness. Growth starts at the top.

A brief note to middle managers:

Implementing some of these initiatives may feel out of reach if you're not in the C-suite or don't control the budget. You might *want* these changes, but lack the authority to call some of the bigger shots. If that's the case, start small. Host a monthly "reflection circle" with your team. Present research to the person you report to about the ROI of EQ training. Partner with another manager who shares your beliefs and brainstorm ideas with them. You may not have full control, but you *do* have influence! Use it wisely. You have the power and you don't need anyone's permission.

Again, I had to cut things to not make this book too long. There's still a lot I wish I could share with you. Scan this QR code for more resources.

Chapter 4: Developing Emotional Intelligence

"Emotional intelligence is not the opposite of intelligence, it is not the triumph of heart over head—it is the unique intersection of both."
— David Caruso

Once you have established a foundational level of self-awareness—where you're beginning to observe and understand your thoughts, behaviors, and emotions—it becomes critical to extend that awareness beyond yourself with emotional intelligence (EQ).

Though many people would consider themselves emotionally intelligent, only about one-third of the global population is adept in this trait. Psychologist Daniel Goleman (2024), a pioneer in the field, outlined four core components to EQ: self-awareness, self-management, social awareness, and relationship management. In other words, emotional intelligence is the ability to understand oneself and others deeply, and to manage emotions and interpersonal dynamics with nuance and strategic foresight. EQ isn't a concept you can fully master through textbooks and lectures; it must be cultivated through deliberate practice.

Emotional intelligence is important because it allows you to develop resilience, utilize vulnerability intentionally, and lead authentically. For EQ to be *strategic*, it requires the capacity to hold space for complexity and contradictions—and to respond with composure rather than impulsivity.

We initiated the discussion on the first component of EQ, self-awareness, in Chapter 3: Cultivating Self-Awareness. This chapter builds on that foundation, integrating additional insights on EQ and the importance of emotional regulation, resilience, and vulnerability. You'll also hear from my personal coach, Michele, whose work has significantly impacted not only how I lead, but how I live my life.

Understanding Emotions

Of course, you understand emotions on a basic level: tears often signal sadness, frowns often signal anger, smiles often signal joy. But it is critical to understand them on a more complex level: that your emotional state directly informs how you show up in any environment. Tone, pace, vocabulary, and nonverbal communication all transmit emotional signals, which carry significant influence even when unspoken. Think of these components as elements of an instrument. What kind of music are you playing? Are you embodying the calm facilitator, the inspiring visionary, or the angry dictator?

If you've never considered this before, start by asking yourself when you walk into a room: "What emotional state am I in right now? How might this state influence those around me? What impressions and signals am I giving?" Emotional intelligence requires this constant curiosity and reflection. If you begin to notice what micro-cues are beneficial or harmful, you can start making changes to how you show up.

With EQ, it's equally as important to be aware of others and their emotions too. Shift these questions to apply to peers when you walk into a room: "What emotional state might they be in? What are their nonverbal cues suggesting? How is their energy impacting the room—and me?" This level of awareness is foundational for beginning to build EQ, because the person who understands and deciphers emotions is the person who can relate and empathize with others.

Be aware, too, as you examine others, that some people use emotional intelligence negatively (think narcissists who are self-serving). Ask yourself in the presence of others: "Do I feel safe with this person? Is their external appearance matching their internal energy? Are they acting fake? Do I feel worse after leaving a conversation with them?" Walk away from emotional vampires, drama queens, and narcissists, who may use emotional intelligence to manipulate you.

Emotional Regulation

Understanding emotions is one feat, but learning to regulate them is another. If we can't manage our emotions, they manage us. Unchecked, they override logic, undermine leadership, and erode trust.

To regulate effectively, you must learn to *pause*. After emotionally charged interactions, incorporate intentional reset rituals: a deep breathing exercise, a walk, a moment of silence, or music that re-centers your mindset. Then, you can walk into your office or the next boardroom meeting with ease, ready to tackle what comes next without lingering emotions weighing you down.

Emotional regulation can also be learned through studying philosophy. Maybe you've heard of Stoicism: a school of thought that emphasizes the importance of managing what you can control (yourself, your thoughts, your actions) and letting go of what you cannot control (essentially everything else). By leading life with stoicism in mind, you can reduce anxiety and experience more joy, as circumstances and outcomes take up less mental energy, and therefore cause less emotional hardship.

Building Resilience

Let's be honest: Business and life are seldom easy. Challenges, failures, and surprises will come, and change remains life's only constant. It's one thing to be able to regulate your emotions in isolated instances; it's another to remain grounded through sustained pressure or repeated setbacks. That's where resilience comes in.

Imagine this scenario: During a morning meeting, a team member makes a disrespectful remark to the CEO, who is simultaneously navigating a personal crisis outside of work. Which type of CEO earns your respect: the one who erupts in frustration or the one who calmly acknowledges the tension and refocuses the conversation? The latter demonstrates emotional mastery. The former, emotional volatility.

Resilience is the ability to *maintain composure* during chaos and turbulence by learning how to channel your emotions productively. You might still cry or show emotions—it just means you know when, how, and with whom to share.

Researcher Brené Brown highlights the importance of the space between a stimulus and response, often quoting a statement attributed to Austrian psychologist Viktor Frankl's philosophy: "In that space is the power of choice, and in our choice is our liberation and growth" (Stillman, 2023). When provoked—intentionally or not—emotionally intelligent leaders don't take the bait. They pause, observe, and respond with *intention* rather than *reaction*.

Embracing Vulnerability

At first glance, vulnerability may appear disconnected from concepts like emotional regulation and EQ, but in reality, it's central to them—especially in high-stakes leadership roles. Because all too often, in the pursuit of composure, many people default to emotional suppression (the opposite of vulnerability). They aim for resilience but end up masking their humanity.

And while they may think they're concealing it well, emotional incongruence is usually visible through physiological cues, like body language and micro expressions, that our mirror neurons and nervous systems naturally detect.

I'm sure you've seen it before: Someone's tone feels off in a meeting or their enthusiasm seems forced. That type of inauthenticity can create unease and diminish someone's credibility.

So, emotional regulation does not mean emotional suppression. It's about alignment and honesty with yourself and others. That means, if you're having a difficult day, it's more effective to express that rather than power through inauthentically. I've told my team on several occasions, "I'm not at my best today. Someone else should lead this." That level of transparency does not diminish your authority—it amplifies it, and it permits others to be honest, too. (When people feel safe, they dare to be great.)

Michele's Story: From Silence to Emotional Mastery

My executive coach, Michele, once shared with me a great metaphor about vulnerability and authenticity: the story of The Velveteen Rabbit. The rabbit becomes real through love, wear, and tear. And the same is true for you. The more you live, struggle, triumph, and keep going—the more real you become to others. And the more trustworthy.

Michele has so much wisdom and emotional intelligence that I had to get her involved in this project, specifically this chapter, to share her moving story with you.

> *I was raised in a home where feelings weren't the focus; being a compliant "good girl" was the goal. As the eldest child of a teenage mother and an alcoholic military father, the early conditioning I learned was this: In order to be safe, you must appear strong. Strength often looked like silence. It looked like not crying. It looked like sucking it up and getting the job done.*
>
> *While this did teach me resilience, it also taught me to deeply suppress my feelings in every area of my life. I don't blame my parents though; they were doing the best they could with what they had. Plus, that initial absence of handling emotions and feelings is vital to my story. Looking back, my life has been one continuous series of emotional intelligence breakthroughs—moments where life cracked me open again and again, and I had no choice but to grow. These moments eventually led me to where I am today: living my purpose.*
>
> *The first stand-out moment that comes to mind happened when I was just a teen. My father, a*

man who had risen from poverty to owning multiple businesses and generating over a million dollars, looked at me and asked, "Mitch, why am I not happy? It's just... I got everything. I got the wife, the kids, the house, the business, the money. I thought that would bring me happiness." I was too young to answer such a weighted question and just stared at him, so badly wishing I could help. It was my first lesson in emotional intelligence: Outward success can distract us from doing the deep inner work, and it doesn't guarantee fulfillment. True fulfillment comes from understanding your emotional needs and defining your own version of success.

Of course, at that age, I couldn't even begin to understand the woes of an adult's life. I was just a kid, and I was not very happy myself. Having been taught not to trust others and not to share emotions left me feeling isolated from my peers.

When I was a sophomore in high school, my dad retired from the military and moved the family to a small town out in the country. Life as I knew it flipped upside down: I could not seem to make friends, so I sat alone at lunch every day and felt totally despondent.

Not wanting to be at school, I escaped into higher learning. Every day at noon I would leave campus to attend community college. I placed at the top of those classes and my instructors would often praise me in front of my older peers. And suddenly, my self-esteem started to blossom. This became my second lesson in emotional intelligence: Self-perception shapes both your confidence and your impact. Rather than contort yourself to fit in, identify and lean into your unique strengths. How you see yourself informs every decision you make—and influences how others perceive you as well.

POWER WITHOUT PERMISSION

During my senior year in high school, I found a brochure for a college in San Diego. It looked to be near a beach, and there were palm trees swaying above the university buildings. It motivated me to apply for college. After all, I hadn't had much encouragement for education elsewhere. I took the SAT exam and, thankfully, my high score combined with my early college courses earned me acceptance into that very college: SDSU School of Business.

While many of my peers in college prioritized their social lives, I, again, poured myself into academics. During a lighthearted dorm award ceremony, where people received titles like "Most Likely to Be Stoned" or "Most Likely to Have Three Girlfriends," I was voted "Most Likely to Graduate." At the time, I found it boring. But years later, as I walked down a campus hallway following graduation, a professor stopped me and said, "Congratulations! You finished first in the School of Business." I was stunned. I hadn't even been trying to be at the top of my class because competition had always made me uncomfortable. Plus, as a girl raised in the 1960s, sports and competition were not encouraged. Winning was not in my vocabulary.

Hence came my third lesson in emotional intelligence: Releasing shame around ambition strengthens self-worth. You are allowed to want success. You are allowed to own your wins. Rewriting unhelpful internal narratives can change the trajectory of your life.

I made use of my degree and owned a few small businesses after a short career in HR. One business succeeded and sold at a healthy profit. Then, during the Great Recession, my next venture failed, leading to significant financial loss and a forced move from California to Illinois. I felt defeated and ashamed, not realizing it was yet another pivotal lesson in emotional intelligence: Resilience grows when we separate events from identity. When something painful happens, you can choose not to make it personal. Emotionally intelligent people know that "failure" is not a reflection of who you are.

This was not something I quite understood at the moment; it would take years and deeper work to reclaim my self-worth from the rubble of that collapse. Truth be told, I stepped away from business for a while after that. My husband provided for us financially while I stayed at home to raise our two daughters. That turned out to be an amazing blessing. The time spent with my daughters brought me joy and wisdom, and motherhood became the best emotional challenge I could ever experience.

Once my daughters reached middle school, and I had more free time, I decided to go back to school for a master's degree. I was accepted into a graduate program at the University of California, Irvine. Life had other plans, though, and I didn't end up doing the program. Just as I was set to begin, I received a call from a doctor. My eldest daughter had a brain tumor and needed immediate surgery or she might die. It knocked my legs out from under me. Though we later learned it was a false alarm, the emotional whiplash was overwhelming. Not long after, my younger daughter faced her own medical crisis, having contracted a parasite and salmonella, and I found myself once again navigating intense fear and helplessness.

Motherhood, especially under such high-stakes pressure, cracked me open emotionally. Two harrowing years of back-to-back medical crises (that felt like ten years) forced me into the deepest surrender of my life. Honestly, I could barely function or get off the couch. Desperate to learn how to manage my emotions and stress, I hired a coach to learn how to regulate my nervous system, recognize emotional triggers, reconnect with my body, and reclaim agency over my internal world. That's when I truly began my emotional mastery journey. I was no longer surviving on resilience, but living with intentional emotional awareness.

During that time, I also had to confront the reality that my marriage was unraveling. My husband and I (who were already different) diverged even more drastically in our values and vision. While I sought healing and therapy, he had already exited emotionally and financially. Though my personal work helped me grow, it couldn't save a relationship that wasn't mutual. It would have been easy to fall into the victim trap, but with the life wisdom I had gained and healing work I had done, I knew better. So, I made a choice. I rejected the trope of the "empty-nest divorcée" with a sad story. Instead, I chose reinvention. I would be a woman with purpose, passion, and power, which led to the greatest breakthrough of all: Motivation is built through clarity, belief, and action. Emotionally intelligent leaders pursue goals by conceiving their purpose, believing in their worth, and taking intentional steps forward to achieve their goals. Yes, it is hard, but it is also doable.

I found my way into an esteemed coaching certification program, the only woman in a cohort of older, very successful men. After graduating, I challenged myself to launch a CEO peer group before any of my peers (this time, not shying away from competition), and I succeeded. Then I launched two more groups, and I haven't looked back since. Executive coaching and peer group facilitation have

> *proved to be the most challenging and rewarding occupations I could imagine. It feels like a calling rather than a job.*
>
> *Every breakthrough from my life path (early emotional suppression, academic excellence, business success and failure, motherhood, trauma, divorce, and reinvention) has led me here. Not just as a coach, but as a woman who knows how to feel, think, and lead with heart. I sometimes work with CEOs who mirror the emotional struggle I first witnessed in my father: "I've checked all the boxes... why am I still unhappy?" I hear those words echoed again and again, but this time I am no longer a silent teenager. And what an honor it is to guide others into their own transformation.*

As Michele's story illustrates, emotional intelligence is vital both personally and professionally; it helps with decision-making, interpersonal relationships, and resilience in the face of adversity. It is the very trait that propelled her life forward again and again, eventually leading her to discover her life purpose and mission, where she experiences *daily fulfillment*.

Activities for Developing EQ

Like anything else, EQ is built through deliberate practice. Try these exercises, and don't move on to the next chapter until you've done them.

#1: Do Emotional Check-Ins:

For one week, reflect on the following questions every time you engage in a certain activity, such as drinking water, taking a shower, or opening your front door. (By tying the check-ins to specific activities, they will be abrupt—naturally teaching you to check in with yourself at random times.)

- What emotions have I experienced recently?
- What triggered them?

- What helped me shift into a better emotional state?

#2: **Start an Observation Log:**

During any upcoming team meetings, observe:

- How are colleagues presenting themselves emotionally?
- Who appears energized? Who seems disengaged?
- How did their presence influence the atmosphere?

#3: **Learn Your Core Values:**

To have emotional intelligence is to deeply know yourself and what you stand for. One of the first questions I ask any mentee or client is, "What are your core values?" The question shouldn't leave you stumped. What do you believe in? What drives you? What values are the most important for you to live by and honor?

#4: **Meditate or Do Yoga:**

Mindfulness practices will help you observe your thoughts and emotions. The more you witness these patterns in action, the more in tune with yourself you will be and the quicker you can dismantle thought patterns that don't serve you.

#5: **Schedule a Debate:**

Get together with a group of friends, colleagues, or trusted peers and choose a topic that invites real thought. It doesn't have to be political or polarizing, but it should matter enough that people care about it. (For example: "Does cancel culture help or harm social progress?") The goal is not to win the debate, but to practice awareness of yourself and others. Observe your emotions. Are you truly listening? Do you feel defensive? Consider others: How are tones shifting? Body language? After the debate, compare and contrast different perspectives purely from a logical lens as if you were a third-party observer. This will help you see beyond your own perspective and hold empathy for others' realities.

Call to Action for Leaders

Consider this: The World Economic Forum (2025) has identified emotional intelligence as one of the top 10 most critical skills for the modern workplace. Yet, a global study conducted by Harvard Business Review in partnership with Four Seasons Hotels found that fewer than 20% of companies can be classified as emotionally intelligent organizations (Bolden-Barrett & Fecto, 2019).

The implication is clear: EQ is necessary, and yet it's a huge blind spot in the world of business. Odds are, you're not currently working at an organization that's adept in EQ, so it's up to you to bring EQ into the picture. When you lead with emotional intelligence, your team will elevate alongside you. Make sure you are doing the following.

#1: Become a Calm Space Maker:

Echoing Brené Brown's insights, leaders must create psychological space by pausing before reacting. When you take the time to intentionally respond, you are modeling reflection for your employees. By showing restraint in emotionally charged moments, you, as the leader, keep the collective space safe and calm. Others will naturally follow your lead.

#2: Deliver EQ-Oriented Feedback:

During team meetings or in one-on-ones, ask reflective, emotionally intelligent questions such as "How do you think your message landed?" or "What were you feeling in that situation?" or "What emotions came up for you the most this week?" to spark curiosity in others.

#3: Be an Active Listener:

Exercise your own EQ by actively listening instead of thinking or talking. This can look like any of the following: ask follow up questions to understand someone's thought process or idea on a deeper level; resist the urge to plan your response or solve a problem while someone is still speaking; paraphrase what you heard to confirm that you understood what was said; pause before answering to give space for deeper reflection or continued sharing.

#4: Listen to Women:

Women are naturally more adept in EQ than men. Listen to the women in your office and their ideas. If men are interrupting women, put an end to it by using respectful but firm language that redirects the conversation. For example: "Let's pause for a moment. I want to make sure we hear where she was going with that." or "Hold on. I'd like to hear her finish her thought first." Remember that the loudest or most aggressive voice shouldn't be the one that wins! (This is another tool to help you be a calm space maker.)

#5: Listen to Introverts:

In my personal experience, I have found some of the most insightful people to be those who are introverted or shy. Those who tend to be quieter or recharge solo often do a good amount of listening. Lean into this. Bring them into a one-on-one and pick their brain. Specifically call on them in meetings for their opinions: "Hey, you have great insights. What do you think about this?"

Scan this QR code for more resources.

Chapter 5: Overcoming the Fear of Judgment

"Everything you want is on the other side of fear." — Jack Canfield

The fear of judgment is one of the most pervasive barriers stopping people from seeking fulfillment—both personally and professionally. It often masquerades as "being practical," "waiting for the right time," or "gaining more experience." But beneath these rational-sounding justifications lies one thing: fear. Not only the fear of failure, but the fear of how others would perceive you or your failure. And this fear can become especially pronounced in the workplace, where expectations are high and everyone's performance is public.

The reality is, you can't and never will earn universal approval. Attempting to do so only dilutes your power, depletes your energy, and distracts you from your purpose. Of course, as human beings, we are wired to seek belonging and acceptance. It's natural to care what others think—but it's a strategic error to let others' opinions dictate your choices or how you show up. Instead, consider others' opinions as their perception—not as fact. When you maintain this boundary, you prevent your biological need for validation from spiraling into what I call "looping": chronic overthinking, hesitation, and self-doubt.

Reflect for a moment: Have you ever found yourself replaying conversations, redrafting emails repeatedly, or envisioning terrible outcomes? Have you shied away from sharing your ideas or declined an opportunity that could have propelled you forward? This is the fear of judgment in action. And you are making these fear-based decisions when 99% of your worst fears never even become reality.

Fortunately, you can navigate this fear by reframing it. In this chapter, we'll explore the nature of judgment, challenge outdated definitions of success and failure, and embrace imperfection. You will also hear Kana's journey—a story of resilience in the face of continuous internal and external judgment.

Understanding Judgment

It may be difficult to accept, but other people's opinions do not determine your value. When you find yourself mentally looping—endlessly analyzing potential critiques or hypothetical scenarios—you are not engaging with reality. Instead, it's like you're engaging with a made-up Netflix series, binge-watching your own fear-based projections: "What if they think I'm not qualified? What if they don't like how I lead? "What if I say the wrong thing? What if I fail and everyone sees it?" I don't know about you, but I'd turn that distracting media off.

What's even crazier is that most people are not preoccupied with you; they're too busy thinking about themselves. And, in the rare instance that someone *is* judging you, that judgment says more about *them and their insecurities* than it does about *you* and *your capabilities*.

I once worked with a client who was deeply affected by the cultural expectations she carried. She constantly assumed that she was being scrutinized by others. But when we unpacked her experience, we discovered that her harshest critic was not the external world—it was her own internal dialogue and projected fears. The issue wasn't others' judgments; it was self-perception. And that is often the case.

Redefining Success and Failure

Take a moment and ponder these questions: How do you define success? Is it a title? A financial milestone? A glowing performance review? Or is it something simpler and more intrinsic—like having enough, feeling purpose, or showing up as your authentic self?

Mainstream narratives have, unfortunately, sold us extremely narrow definitions. Success is relentless achievement. Failure is rejection. But these rigid metrics are outdated. They don't serve ambitious businesswomen, or anyone, for that matter—which is why we need to reframe them. Success can mean many things: initiating something new, keeping a promise to yourself, or courageously sharing your viewpoint. Failure, by contrast, has only one definition: choosing comfort over growth. And rejection isn't failure! It should be seen as redirection and an opportunity for learning and growth.

Let me paint this in an example: Susie applied for a role and, after an initial interview, was told she wasn't the right fit. Did she fail? Not at all. I'd argue that she succeeded. She put herself out there, took initiative, and made room for alignment elsewhere.

When you release societal standards, you not only liberate yourself from others' opinions but gain the freedom to follow your internal compass.

Embracing Imperfections

One of the most dangerous myths I've come across is the belief that confidence must precede action. In truth, the opposite is more accurate: Action generates confidence. You don't need to feel ready, be sure of yourself, or have all the answers. You only need to show up and begin—and if you stop, then start again, and again, and again.

Progress, leadership, and confidence are not *prerequisites*—they are *results*. Progress is built through practice. Leadership is forged through action—even when it's imperfect. Confidence is gained through trials and tribulations.

And that is why it is vital to embrace imperfection and take imperfect action. In fact, showing vulnerability and owning what you don't know can cultivate trust and authenticity. People gravitate toward what is real, not what is flawless—because real is relatable. And if your workplace punishes vulnerability or authenticity, it may be a sign to reassess whether it's the right environment for you. (We'll explore this further in Chapter 6: Navigating Power Dynamics and Office Politics.)

ANDREAS PETTERSSON

Kana's Story: When the Real Judge Lived Within

Take Kana, for example: When I hired her, I saw her potential before she fully did. She tended to minimize her achievements and struggled to see herself as a leader. However, despite these internal challenges, she kept showing up and stepping out of her comfort zone. Eventually, she became grounded in confidence. But her skills didn't just magically appear—they were built over time, choice by choice, action by action.

> *I was born in Japan and immigrated to the United States when I was five years old. While my family adapted to American society externally—navigating the school system and integrating into our new community—our home remained deeply rooted in Japanese culture, values, and expectations. The contrast between my home life and the world outside was something I had to grapple with at a very young age.*
>
> *One of the earliest and most enduring challenges I faced was the language barrier. In the classroom, I often struggled to keep up with what was being said, and on the playground, I couldn't always understand the kids I was trying to befriend. At times, I felt like my peers might have even been picking on me. I became hyper-aware of how I was being perceived—wondering constantly, Did I say that right? Are they laughing at me?*
>
> *Even as I became more fluent, that initial insecurity planted a long-lasting fear: the fear of judgment, which silently followed me for years. In high school, I vividly remember showing up quiet, hesitant, and intimidated in social circles—which is ironic considering I belonged to a very prominent group as a strong athlete and captain of the cheerleading team.*

POWER WITHOUT PERMISSION

This fear wasn't just confined to school or social settings—it pervaded every aspect of my life, even following me home. My brother, just a year and a half older than me, was exceptionally bright. He attended prestigious universities that were well known in our home country of Japan—UCLA and USC—while I attended UCSB and later UCI, schools that my extended family had never heard of. Although these are excellent schools, I still internalized the comparison and interpreted it as further evidence that I was falling short. Even though no one in my family ever outwardly expressed judgment, I still saw myself as the "less intelligent" sibling, despite my own academic strengths.

At UCSB, I pursued a degree in Mathematics—a subject I excelled in. But like many in their teens and early twenties, I wasn't entirely sure what I wanted to do with my life. After graduating, I found myself drawn to data and coding and became intrigued by the idea of engineering, though it felt intimidating. Nevertheless, I made the decision to return to school and pursue a Master's in Computer Science at UCI.

Those two years were some of the most challenging of my life. Coming from a math background, I lacked some of the foundational computer science experience my peers had. Thankfully, I had classmates who helped me study and understand the concepts I struggled with. But even still, I felt perpetually behind, overwhelmed, and deeply unsure of myself. The stress was so intense that I even began losing hair from anxiety. A single thought constantly echoed through my mind: I can't fail. Not because of grades or pride—but because I feared what failure would mean. Failure would confirm every hidden doubt: that I didn't measure up to my brother, that my parents had sacrificed for nothing, that I didn't belong in a field for "smart people."

Toward the end of my studies, I got an internship at Andreas' company doing data labeling. My confidence was at an all-time low. I constantly questioned my worth: Anyone could do this. What do I bring to the table? All the while, I failed to acknowledge my strongest trait: my ability to learn. I eagerly absorbed information from those around me and began building the skills necessary to contribute meaningfully.

When Andreas offered me a full-time position, I hesitated. I didn't understand what he saw in me, and I didn't feel like I knew what I was doing. When we discussed salary, I lowballed myself—asking for $60,000. He ended up offering more because my ask was far below what was appropriate.

Still unsure of myself, I accepted the role—and the title—of Data Engineer. I didn't understand what exactly that meant, and I still felt unworthy. I stuck with that title for an entire year because I was too afraid to ask for a title change. Eventually, a colleague said that my title didn't make sense, and that's when it changed to Software Engineer. Both my father and brother are engineers, and I had spent my entire life admiring their intelligence and ability. The idea that I could belong in a similar professional category seemed absurd. Despite earning my place, I couldn't accept or celebrate it.

For a couple of years, I worked diligently, striving to match the level of my peers, never quite believing the truth: I was already there. I even got promoted to Senior Software Engineer. And yet, I dismissed the achievement. I assumed it happened only because the previous senior had left—not because I had demonstrated leadership or expertise. I couldn't admit to myself that I had earned it, just like I couldn't fully accept that I had earned my role as cheer captain years before. I told myself it was circumstantial, not personal merit.

I realize now, though, that it wasn't a lack of ability—it was fear. Fear made it nearly impossible to internalize success. The fear of judgment. The fear of disappointment. The fear of disapproval. The fear of not meeting expectations. And that fear was the very thing that, paradoxically, pushed me forward for much of my career. I was constantly trying to earn my place again and again, which exhausted me and spread me thin—because fear never lets you rest. It always finds something wrong with what you're doing.

Even within the industry, there's an unwritten rule that engineers should switch companies every few years to secure higher pay. Despite being newly promoted and happy where I was, I felt pressure to conform. I applied elsewhere and received an offer. The only thing is, it would have been a step down in title. I grappled with what to do: stay on an atypical route or leave for a demotion? I felt I'd receive judgment with either decision. Colleagues advised me to stay, and ultimately I did, but it's telling that I even considered leaving.

Soon after, I was promoted again—this time to Lead Senior Software Engineer. It was in this role that something shifted. As if I realized it could no longer be a coincidence that I was succeeding. I began to see the value I brought, and the respect I had earned, beginning my journey of unlearning the inner narrative that had plagued me for so long.

For the first time, I wasn't propelled by comparison or pressure—I was driven by purpose. My father and brother, who had once felt like benchmarks, now felt like peers, and I was no longer "just the younger sibling." In fact, today my family regularly turns to me for help—my dad for work advice, my mom for support with English. At some point during one of these exchanges, I finally realized: The fear of judgment I carried for so long was often just an untrue story I was telling myself.

In retrospect, I see how vital every life chapter has been. For example, my graduate school experience—grueling as it was—taught me perseverance. And more than any natural ability or technical skill, that is what has carried me to where I am today, with a title I never could have imagined for myself. I didn't always feel equipped. I wasn't always confident. But I kept going. I asked for help. I leaned on others. I gave myself permission to learn and grow beyond wherever I was.

If there's one insight I can leave you with, it's this: Fear is rarely about something external—it's about your internal story. So, if you fear judgment, fear failing, or fear what comes next, know that you don't have to wait until you're confident to take the next step. Move forward anyway. Surround yourself with those who support your growth. And above all, trust that your voice, potential, and path are worth following.

What I deeply admire about Kana's story is her ability to take action in spite of fears, doubts, and worries. Even more powerful was the shift she made from letting fear drive her to letting purpose lead her. Fear will always try to shrink us—and if we let it, it will. Kana is living proof of what becomes possible when we move through fear: career success, personal growth, and strengthened bonds.

Activities for Overcoming the Fear of Judgment

Having a fear of judgment may never fully disappear, but you can change your relationship to it. (Whenever fear appears in my own life, I lean into the feeling and embrace the experience as a learning or growth opportunity.) Fear shouldn't always be seen as a red flag—sometimes it's a green light urging you toward new possibilities and the unknown. Remember: You are not here to be admired by everyone. You are here to live a life of integrity and courage. That means taking risks and allowing yourself to be seen.

Just like Kana, you have the power to move forward even in the presence of fear. Fear is not waiting to give you permission. Start by trying these activities. Don't move on to the next chapter until you've done them.

#1: Journal Your Definitions:

Reflect on and write down your past definitions of success, failure, judgment, and rejection. Then, write out new definitions for each word. Think: "What definitions would be the most helpful and motivating for me?" Whenever you feel yourself slipping into outdated beliefs, revisit these notes.

#2: Partner Reflection:

Explore this question with someone you trust: "Why is being disliked difficult for me to accept? What do I believe it says about me?" Then challenge those answers together. (It likely stems from an outdated belief from when you were younger. Challenge yourself to embrace who you are now— not the old versions of you. It's time to move forward!)

#3: Take Immediate Action:

Identify one task or decision you've delayed due to fear of judgment—and take microactions today. It doesn't matter if it's small or big. Just begin. Don't wait to feel ready. This is how we can make the unfamiliar familiar: by stepping into it.

#4: Examine Your Behavior:

Have you heard of "above the line" and "below the line" behaviors? Above-the-line behaviors are positive and constructive. Below-the-line behaviors are negative and negative. If you're constantly operating from your fears and worries, you're engaging in below-the-line behavior. When you catch yourself, pause, and remind yourself to rise above the line.

#5: Tally Your Time:

Count how many times (or how many minutes) you spend worrying, feeling fear, or replaying the past in a single day. No matter your results, try to get that number down the following day. Or, designate a set time for worrying—like Mondays from 8:00 a.m. to 8:30 a.m.—and let go of worrying outside that time window. Try this intentionally for a week.

Call to Action for Leaders

The fear of judgment isn't just a personal obstacle—it's a systemic issue, often intertwined with broader struggles like anxiety or depression that shape organizational culture in profound ways. While mental health issues can arise from many factors beyond the fear of judgment alone, a culture steeped in criticism or lacking safety only makes things worse.

According to the Anxiety & Depression Association of America (2006), 56% of employees report that anxiety negatively impacts their performance at work, 51% say it negatively affects coworker relationships, and 43% say it strains their relationship with leadership. Alarmingly, many employees revealed that they cope not with constructive tools but with caffeine, alcohol, nicotine, or prescription medications.

This data should serve as a wake-up call. As a leader, it's your responsibility to dismantle the culture of fear by fostering psychological safety, encouraging self-expression, and normalizing conversations about mental health. Make sure you're doing the following:

#1: Allow for Feedback:

Create space for team members to share ideas and concerns. This invites input from more reserved voices who may hesitate to speak up. (Emphasize the importance of keeping feedback constructive and "above the line.")

#2: Normalize Mental Health Conversations:

Regularly discuss topics like impostor syndrome, fear of judgment, and workplace anxiety. (Use this book as a guide.) Encourage your team to reflect, journal, and grow alongside you. This builds trust and creates a healthier workplace.

#3: Set Up One-on-One Meetings:

Schedule regular check-ins with each team member individually. Use this time not only to discuss work but also to connect on a more personal level—within professional boundaries. Create space for authentic conversation, allowing the employee's full humanity to be seen and valued.

#4: Look for Diamonds in the Rough:

I recognized instantly that Kana was a diamond in the rough—despite her fears. You, too, have diamonds around you. Are you missing their potential because you aren't seeing what lies behind their fear? Take a closer look at your employees. Find the diamonds and invest in them.

#5: Promote Self-Compassion:

Many people who fear judgment struggle with self-compassion. Encourage employees to be kind to themselves—and model it in your own behavior to lead by example.

ANDREAS PETTERSSON

Scan this QR code to check out more resources.

Quick Pause — Are you enjoying this book so far?

I have a small ask for you that will make a big impact. If you've made it this far and you're feeling inspired, learning something new, or simply enjoying the growth journey, would you take a moment to leave a review on Amazon?

Your words matter more than you know—think of all the times you've picked up a book based on reviews and ratings. Leaving a review won't just support me as the author—it will help the book find its way into the hands of the women, men, and leaders who truly need it. The entrepreneurs, the go-getters, the growth-oriented, and the finally-ready-to-change—those who may need these words, these chapters, or these sections just as much as you did.

You might not directly see the effects of taking two minutes to share your thoughts, but that doesn't mean something powerful won't come from it. You're not just leaving a review—you're spreading the word about a book that can help someone else heal, grow, and thrive.

Thanks for being a part of this mission. You're a diamond.

Scan the QR code to leave a review.

Section III: Direction & Action
Locate and Make the Initial Cuts

Chapter 6: Navigating Power Dynamics and Office Politics

"If you have some power, then your job is to empower somebody else."
— Toni Morrison

At a certain point in every development journey, growth must expand beyond the internal—your mindset, habits, and beliefs—and extend into how you engage with others. While Section II: Awareness focused on mastering the internal game, Section III: Direction and Action is about mastering the external game with equal finesse. In this context, the external refers to workplace culture and the broader organizational environment. My intention is that the insights and practices gained from the previous section will empower you to step into this next phase with courage and readiness.

We'll begin with a topic that is both highly influential and universally experienced in the workplace: power dynamics and office politics—the places where the most paramount decisions and opportunities lie. Professional success rarely hinges on competence alone; it is equally dependent on your ability to navigate the subtle and complex networks of power and influence.

Some of you might be yawning or ready to skip to the next chapter, believing that power and politics have no purpose and getting involved won't suit you. But the truth is, declaring yourself "non-political" is, paradoxically, a political act in itself. Whether you like it or not, hierarchies—both formal and informal—exist in every institution, from family systems to corporate offices to social structures. Humans are naturally driven to create them.

It's time to let go of the illusion that diligence and humility alone are enough. Keeping your head down, working hard, and hoping good things will come is not a strategy. It's a path to failure. Ignoring power structures will simply leave you vulnerable to those who understand and leverage them.

For example, according to a recent survey by LendingTree, only 35% of women ask for promotions, while 49% of men do (Pope, 2024). So while it's true that there is a gender pay gap (I'm not denying that!), part of the issue can be addressed if more women start asking for pay raises.

What I'm saying is, immersing yourself in the systems that exist is the path to reaching your highest potential. And that doesn't mean accepting sexism or abandoning the fight for change. It means participating with clarity, confidence, and strategy.

Defining Power and Politics in the Workplace

For many women, the phrase *office politics* conjures negative connotations—manipulation, hidden agendas, power grabs. It's no surprise, given that politics has long been seen as a "dirty" word, associated with inauthenticity and self-interest.

But here's the truth: Politics isn't the problem—*how* people engage in politics is. What we often mistake for "politics" is actually different forms of drama: gossip, triangulation, emotional reactivity, and immaturity. These behaviors create toxic environments full of mistrust and volatility.

Take, for example, the television series *House of Cards*, which paints an extreme world where power is pursued for its own sake through deceit, coercion, and betrayal. While fictional and dramatized, it does tap into a real-world truth: Power and politics are always present in professional environments.

But they don't have to be corrosive—so it's time we redefine office politics.

When approached with ethics and integrity, office politics are neutral—something that naturally exists and must be navigated. It's about understanding who holds power, how power is exercised, and how you want to position yourself. You want to cultivate relationships built on mutual support and align yourself with leaders who lead with integrity and authenticity.

And rest assured that those who rely on performative charm or aggressive tactics will eventually erode their own credibility and meet their demise. Three words about fake people: Eventually. Everyone. Knows.

You can avoid being pulled into toxic spaces by setting clear, professional boundaries with those engaging in unhealthy politics. For example, when someone starts gossiping, ask: "Have you addressed this directly with the person you're speaking about?" If they say no, simply respond: "Then I'd suggest you speak with them first. After that, I'm open to discussing it."

This simple boundary protects your integrity and discourages dysfunction. (Cough, cough—this is engaging in politics in a healthy way, influencing culture, standing firm on values, and positioning oneself as a grounded leader.)

Understanding Power

Social power is having the ability to influence others, and it can come from a variety of sources: expertise (informational power), the ability to reward or penalize (reward or coercive power), or one's position in the hierarchy (legitimate power). Regardless of its source, what matters is how you choose to wield it.

I've worked with many women who are hesitant to identify as "powerful," associating power with aggression or manipulation. But true power is not loud, domineering, or aggressive. It is being grounded—both verbally and physically.

Verbally, it means staying composed, steady, and rooted in self-assurance. Physically, it means adopting open, expansive postures: chest open, shoulders back, eyes steady, feet grounded. After all, how you physically present yourself influences not only how others perceive you, but how you perceive yourself.

Consider this example: Tanya is in the midst of an important meeting when she receives news of a family emergency. Her past instinct would have been to apologize profusely or request permission to step away. Instead, drawing on her recent self-development work, she calmly states, "Something's come up with my child. I'll need to keep my phone nearby in case my husband calls," maintaining eye contact with her manager, her chest and shoulders open.

Notice the shift? No apology. No dramatics. No uncertainty.

So, don't apologize when you haven't done anything wrong. Be direct. Be firm.

Dealing with Resistance

What differentiates those who advance from those who plateau is not the absence of opposition, but the ability to remain composed in the face of it. Resistance is inevitable. If you speak your truth or challenge the status quo, someone will resist. The question is: Will you remain calm, or will you crumble?

Far too often, I've witnessed talented professionals—especially women—enter high-stakes spaces and freeze when others exert dominance. They feel like asserting their needs is selfish. They confuse harmony with being silent. They worry that saying "I" will make them seem arrogant or self-centered. And so, they crumble—sometimes, especially around men who represent a dominant, angry father figure.

We just talked about the importance of facing fear in the last chapter—now it's time to apply it. Don't let your fears and worries make you stagnant.

In reality, owning your voice and articulating your value is what earns respect and commands attention. So the next time you're confronted with hostile dominance, whether it's a raised voice, a challenge of your credibility, or stirred-up drama—resist the urge to mirror that energy. Pause. Breathe. Remain grounded. Sit up straight. Respond calmly.

One of the most effective strategies I've developed over fifteen years in business is simple: Arrive prepared—with facts, clarity, and humility. When someone attempts to discredit or distort the narrative, it doesn't work. Why? Because I've built a reputation on integrity. I've already acknowledged my missteps, spoken transparently, and stayed aligned with the truth.

Facts are disarming. They neutralize corrupt agendas.

Cheryl's Story: From Proving Herself to Empowering Herself

If there's one woman whose story you can learn from when it comes to office politics and power dynamics, it's my colleague Cheryl. She experienced immense workplace trauma with a female manager, and the lessons and transformations that came out of her experience were remarkable.

> *I was raised in a large Italian Catholic household, the eldest of five children—four girls and one boy. That role alone came with unspoken yet distinct expectations only eldest daughters can understand, shaping how I showed up in the world and how I internalized my place within it.*
>
> *Around freshman year of high school, my parents divorced, and I chose to live with my dad. It made sense at the time—he was both my coach and mentor, and I had always been academically and athletically gifted. But that decision planted early seeds of pressure and perfectionism—patterns that would later shape how I navigated relationships, power dynamics, and the constant need to prove myself.*
>
> *Our relationship was challenging for a few years, mostly due to my being an insecure, anxious overachiever who felt like I could never meet my dad's extremely high expectations. If I got an A on a test, he'd ask why it wasn't an A+. If I scored four goals in a soccer game, he'd point out the opportunity for a fifth goal that I passed up for an assist. This never came from a place of cruelty—he recognized my*

capability and was determined to help me reach my potential. But it embedded deeply within my brain chemistry a drive to constantly chase the next achievement. It taught me that I was the only person holding myself back from greatness. Unfortunately, it also meant I never felt good enough. I was constantly seeking validation from others.

I'm grateful to say that today, my dad and I are very close, and it's now obvious he's always been my biggest fan and supporter. Nevertheless, my upbringing bred in me a powerful drive to overperform, to overachieve, and—more insidiously—to please. I became what many would call a high-functioning, anxious perfectionist. In many ways, that propelled my early success.

I pursued a degree in psychology, driven by deep curiosity about human behavior, cognition, and emotional dynamics. That academic foundation ultimately led me into Human Resources: a profession that marries business with behavioral insight. I excelled in it, eventually earning a Master's in Human Resources Management.

Throughout my career, I've worked across diverse industries, organizations, and leadership teams. Almost all of my CEOs said I brought an irreplaceable brand of HR to their company—somehow always managing to protect the needs of the business while simultaneously elevating culture and engagement. I was consistently seen as dependable, competent, and respected by supervisors and colleagues alike. And I was always "on."

I was just the kind of employee who went above and beyond—often to a fault. One former manager even asked me to stop overperforming because the team couldn't keep up the same level of service when I was on vacation. At the time, I took it *as a compliment. I didn't yet realize she was helping to highlight a dangerous imbalance within myself: the relentless drive to over-deliver at the expense of my own well-being.*

Everything shifted when I found myself working under a CEO who, quite frankly, I could not please. No matter what I did, I couldn't win her approval or make her happy. She micromanaged every detail, rejected even my strongest work, and subtly undermined my contributions. Already predisposed to overperform, I doubled my efforts—only to feel more invisible and inadequate.

I spent every day riddled with stress, questioning my abilities and worth, losing sleep, and quietly unraveling. What made it even more painful was that I admired her. She was a CEO in a position of influence I aspired to. Someone I wanted to learn from and be mentored by. Instead, I became a casualty of her control: a robotic "yes" woman and "sorry" woman all rolled into one.

Certain I'd impress her with my first major assignment, I organized weeks' worth of work into a concise executive summary and confidently presented it in our weekly one-on-one. While I was mid-sentence, she took control of my computer, scrolled for a moment, and through a deep sigh, uttered these words verbatim: "Cheryl, when I hired you I didn't think I'd need to do your job for you." (And yes, I still sometimes hear those words in my nightmares.) She offered no recommendations or constructive feedback. Just the implication that what I'd prepared wasn't good enough and had to be redone.

That moment triggered a desperate need for her validation—a familiar feeling from childhood. Despite not being able to send a simple email without her approval (which often meant removing a comma or replacing one word with a synonym), I interpreted her need for control as a way of elevating me to her level.

Soon, there were no professional boundaries, but I respected her so much that I convinced myself it would be worth the sacrifice.

When she wasn't able to set the alarm for the office building after working late one evening, I sat on the phone with her for hours, troubleshooting with the security company—even though my phone presence was totally unnecessary. On Christmas Eve, I stayed online with her all day, continuing a project for which my efforts ultimately went unacknowledged. When colleagues worked through illness or didn't use their vacation time, she praised them for being "in it to win it." And that's what I wanted to be. In trying to become the person I thought she would respect, I became someone my loved ones didn't even recognize.

One day, my husband sat me down and confessed that my job was hurting our family and disrupting the peace in our home. I was defensive at first. I thought these were the sacrifices I needed to make to reach my manager's level of success. But after a few more candid conversations and some deep introspection, it finally hit me: My relationship with this woman mirrored the very struggle I faced as a child—desperate to be, not just "good enough," but "the best." Only now, I wasn't a kid. I was a new mother to a young daughter. And suddenly, my actions weren't just shaping my life—they were shaping hers... I didn't want to pass down this legacy of people-pleasing and self-erasure. So, I began the deep—often painful—process of untangling trauma. I committed to healing both myself and the generations of women who would follow me.

Honestly, I should've left that job sooner. After two years, my mental health was frayed. I was diagnosed with obsessive-compulsive disorder and generalized anxiety disorder. And when I started my next role—this time under a compassionate and insightful leader—I showed signs of post-traumatic stress.

My new manager, Andreas, quickly recognized I had been emotionally bruised. He became a mentor who modeled healthy leadership. His trust and support allowed me to begin reclaiming my sense of self. Any time I was triggered, I reminded myself: That woman is no longer in charge of me. That chapter is over.

There's a second learning in this story that is more revealing about how women are treated and perceived systemically. Not long ago, a female friend and colleague asked me if I'd often encountered these complex power dynamics between women in the workplace. She listed numerous negative experiences she'd had with female leaders, expressing her frustrations with women who compete—but I quickly challenged her assertion.

Then, I could see the proverbial light bulb go off.

Men's positions aren't often threatened because there's plenty of room for them in leadership roles. At a table full of leaders, you rarely see more than one woman—if any at all. That scarcity is what creates the competition and fuels the unspoken (and unfair) message among women: "There's only room for one of us. And it's going to be me." So rather than blaming individual women, we need to name the real culprit: the system we were born into.

This is not to say all female leaders behave poorly. I've had extraordinary female mentors who uplifted me and advocated for work–life balance, well-being, and mutual success. But the systemic issue remains: Women are often held to impossible and contradictory standards. In business, don't compete with one another—but just know there's only room for one of you. With family, if you choose work, you're selfish. If you stay home with your kids, you lack ambition. If you prioritize yourself, you're selfish. If you prioritize others, you're weak. No matter the context, the bar is constantly shifting—and never truly within reach.

For the most part, I'm at peace with the path I've taken. But there are days I wonder, "Would I be further along in my career if I hadn't endured that toxic dynamic?" Perhaps. Still, I know that experience—painful as it was—unearthed a deeper truth within me. It became the catalyst for my healing, growth, and empowerment. Today, when I encounter subtle manipulation, passive aggression, or professional jealousy, I recognize it instantly for what it is—and refuse to absorb it. I know my value. I no longer require external validation to confirm it. These days, I remind myself: This is my life. I choose to live with integrity, joy, and freedom. I won't surrender that. And I don't need anyone's permission to claim it.

Now, with two decades in the field, a dual foundation in psychology and HR, and firsthand experience navigating these dynamics, I'm writing a book for women—especially mothers—who need a reminder of their power and permission to choose happiness. I believe deeply in the possibility of a workplace where women lift as they climb. Success is not a zero-sum game. There is enough for all of us. We must support one another, not compete in silence. We must offer grace, not unattainable standards. We must lead with abundance, not scarcity. Because the way we lead today speaks directly to our daughters—and their daughters.

To any woman currently dealing with office politics or power struggles—especially from another woman—please hear this: Your worth is not negotiable. Your talent is not disposable. Your personhood is not defined by others' opinions. If the environment you're in makes you doubt your worth, it's time to walk away. No job is worth your peace of mind, your identity, or your well-being.

And one final note: Never place someone on a pedestal just because they outrank you professionally. A title does not make someone morally or emotionally superior. A few months ago, I ran into that female CEO—my former manager—at a grocery store. We were both with our children. She was pleasant and friendly. I thought, "This is the woman who used to haunt my thoughts? Whose approval I once sacrificed myself for?"

Just like in The Wizard of Oz, the curtain had been pulled back—and there was no wizard. Only a fellow human. Equal. Flawed. And no longer in control of my narrative.

A Deeper Psychological Look

Cheryl's challenges were not indicative of incompetence. Rather, they were the result of her superior's distorted relationship with control—a dynamic more common than we like to admit. Many leaders, both male and female, who are competitive or high-achieving—especially those who've succeeded in structured systems like sports or academia—are unaware of how their standards can alienate and suppress those around them. They often inadvertently lead from fear, not support. And wherever fear exists, power becomes distorted.

Her manager likely believed that, to some extent, she was helping Cheryl. But rather than leading, she was demanding picky results through micromanagement and perfectionism—both of which are signs of leadership insecurity. Once you understand the psychology underneath these power struggles, you can stop personalizing them. And when you stop personalizing them, you can respond with strategy instead of shame—shame that often stems from old patterns and childhood experiences (in this case, Cheryl's manager representing Cheryl's father).

The Importance of Culture

Culture goes deeper than the fluffy aspects of business like brand colors and annual company picnics; it's the invisible engine running the entire organization. It's the values, beliefs, and behaviors that surround you every day, shape how you show up, and inform the unspoken and unwritten rules of the work environment.

If you've ever worked under a leader who needed to be the loudest voice in the room or punished dissenting opinions, then you know this firsthand: Fear-based environments don't produce greatness. They produce compliance. Team members learn to stay quiet, walk on eggshells, fake a smile, feel small, and hide their true selves—because they can't show up authentically.

A healthy culture, on the other hand, is built on psychological safety. It's one where team members feel safe to speak up, disagree, be bold, be wrong, and—most importantly—be real. When people feel safe to be their authentic selves, it creates a domino effect: from curiosity to creativity to innovation. And that's what makes meaningful impact possible.

That's why the best leaders don't lead through intimidation or ego. They lead through presence, empathy, and vision, lifting their employees emotionally—from fear to pride, from defensiveness to courage, from burnout to empowerment. Great leaders will also create environments that are self-adjusting—cultures where toxicity and unhealthy politics are shut down at the source, where judgment isn't tolerated, where everyone is expected to protect one another's dignity.

In Chapter 3: Cultivating Self-Awareness, I mentioned to leaders the importance of fostering a culture that is psychologically safe. While that is the duty and goal for those in leadership positions, it is your job (no matter what position you find yourself in) to decide whether or not the work environment you surround yourself in every day is worth your time and deserving of your energy. Because culture plays a role in your professional development. You could have all the potential in the world, but if the environment is rooted in control, comparison, or quiet competition, you'll plateau—or worse, shrink. So ask yourself: Are questions welcomed where I work? Do I feel safe to express myself authentically? Are differing opinions respected? Are there women in leadership positions—and if there aren't, are others uncomfortable with you asking why not? Your answers to these questions will tell you whether or not your work culture is psychologically safe. If it isn't, then it's time to thoughtfully consider your next steps, because there are more options than simply staying stuck.

First, it's important to take an honest look inward to see if part of the problem is your own patterns, fears, and unspoken expectations. Then, you might consider having direct conversations, setting stronger boundaries, or finding ways to transform what you can of the culture through your own influence. Maybe for you the best option will be to stay, at least for now, to work on your emotional intelligence and resilience. Or the correct decision might be to leave, recognizing that the environment truly can't support your growth. All of these are valid paths. The key is to explore your options with awareness and intention, rather than defaulting to reaction or resignation.

Activities for Navigating Power Dynamics and Office Politics

As you saw with Cheryl, she eventually found her voice again, and it came back even stronger. While working together, I watched her confidence grow, her body language shift, her tone change, and her sense of ownership strengthen. That's the power of reclaiming your voice—and your authentic self.

And remember, your goal is not to win every confrontation. It's to play the long game with integrity. Try these activities to help you get started. Don't move on to the next chapter until you've done them. Please, I'm serious.

#1: Power Posture Drill:

Practice open, confident postures. Stand or sit with shoulders relaxed, spine straight, and eyes forward. Hold for two minutes. Observe the internal shift.

#2: Truth Script:

Identify one situation where you've shrunk or over-apologized. Close your eyes and relive that moment—but this time, come from a place of authority and confidence. If it helps, write down the new version. Then, next time you face a similar situation, draw from this.

#3: Conflict Reframe:

The next time someone gives you resistance, pause and ask yourself, "Is this about me—or about their fear?" Then ask, "What if the opposite of my emotional reaction were true?" Respond with curiosity instead of defensiveness.

#4: Don't Fall Behind:

When walking with peers, managers, or senior leaders into a room, don't trail behind. Walk in first. Lead with your presence—it sends a powerful signal of confidence and personal authority.

#5: Identify Personalities that Scare You:

Every so often, you will come across someone in your personal or professional life whose presence unsettles you or triggers discomfort. Use your self-awareness to pause and ask: "What exactly about this person is making me uncomfortable?" Once you name it, you can shift your internal experience—by setting a boundary, grounding yourself, or choosing to respond rather than react.

(For example, if a coworker consistently corrects your ideas in front of others, you can calmly reclaim your voice by saying, "I was approaching the situation from a different angle, and I believe I have a valid point.")

Call to Action for Leaders

You're in a tough spot because you can't control everything around you. You can't control what happens when you're not in the room. You can't control how another leader chooses to lead. You can't control people's perceptions, fears, or insecurities.

But you *can* control yourself. And at the very least, you can influence the energy in the room to combat toxic dynamics and office politics. Here's where to start:

#1: Self-Audit:

Honestly answer the following questions. Does your workplace environment feel chaotic, unstable, or tense? Is there high turnover, disengagement, or low morale? Do you tend to assign blame to individual employees first? Have you ever considered that you might be part of the problem? Are you showing up as the kind of leader you once needed? Leadership isn't just about guiding—it's also about taking ownership.

#2: Be Inclusive and Transparent:

Promote inclusion by making intentional space for those who are frequently interrupted or overlooked. Practice transparency by communicating clearly and giving direct feedback. When you lead this way, you create a trusting environment where others will follow you—and that's how culture changes.

#3: Call Out Win–Lose Behavior:

If someone in the organization bends the truth (e.g., gossips often or highlights their own wins while emphasizing others' losses), address it directly. Ask them "What is your intent?" or say "I don't understand what you are saying. Can you explain? It seems like you are trying to say something else." You can even encourage them to reframe the way they talk about something: "We didn't get the result we wanted, but here's what I learned and what I'll do differently next time." It's essential to call out their behavior because if gone unchecked, it will breed toxicity and unhealthy political games.

And remember: If someone undermines others once, it may be a mistake. Twice, it's questionable. Three times? It's a pattern. And they may be a cultural liability.

#4: Fire Toxic People:

A toxic person creates unhealthy political dynamics. They may gossip, withhold information, manipulate dynamics, or create tension behind the scenes. These individuals rarely change—but they *do* impact everyone else by contributing to a culture of fear and instability. If you don't let them go, you send a message that toxicity is tolerated as long as results are delivered, and this will erode your credibility. No matter how talented they are, they're worth replacing for the health of the team and your own peace of mind.

#5: Encourage Collaboration:

Collaboration breaks down power imbalances by creating a sense of shared ownership. It promotes innovation and brings diverse perspectives into the room. Create cross-functional projects that involve employees across different levels of hierarchy. (In flatter cultures like Scandinavia, this may come more naturally. In more hierarchical ones, like the U.S., it often requires deliberate effort.)

POWER WITHOUT PERMISSION

Scan this QR code to check out more resources.

Chapter 7: Setting Boundaries and Commanding Respect

"Our boundaries define our personal space — and we need to be sovereign there in order to be able to step into our full power and potential."
— Jessica Moore

Let's talk about boundaries. I know—just hearing the word may make you cringe a little. Boundaries can be hard to implement, but I need you to stick with me. Because here's the truth: If you don't define your boundaries, someone else will—and you probably won't like where they draw the line.

Boundaries are the clear limits you set to protect your time, energy, and well-being. They are simply your way of saying, "This is how I expect to be treated." And setting them doesn't make you difficult, selfish, or rude; setting them is an act of self-respect and a declaration of self-worth. So, whether you're leading a team, negotiating a deal, or simply trying to get through your morning without being interrupted for the hundredth time, setting boundaries is a critical professional skill.

According to the Thriving Center of Psychology, 58% of people report difficulty with saying "no," and 63% of people consider themselves to be people pleasers (2022). And let's be honest—if around 60% *admitted to these things*, that number is likely higher. So, why do so many of us, especially women, struggle with this? Boundary-setting requires one fundamental belief: that you are worth protecting and vouching for. And that, right there, is the heart of this chapter: your worthiness. We'll be diving into boundary setting and work-life integration, and hear from my colleague Stephanie, who transitioned from "overwhelmed and taken advantage of" to "confident and commanding respect."

Recognizing Your Worth

Before you can set boundaries that stick, you need to believe that you are worthy of having them in the first place. Because when you don't value your time, energy, or emotional bandwidth, you'll say yes to every demand, every late-night email, every unreasonable request from the colleague who always dumps their work on you—even when it chips away at your well-being.

Not sure if this applies to you? Let's do a quick self-audit:

- You apologize frequently, even when you've done nothing wrong.
- You stay silent to avoid conflict.
- You allow others to cross your limits because saying "no" feels uncomfortable.
- You put others' needs ahead of your own (most, if not all, of the time).
- You avoid difficult conversations because you fear being disliked.

If most of these sound familiar, pause and breathe. You're not alone and you're not broken. You're human—and likely operating from outdated programming. The good news? You have the power to unlearn and relearn.

True self-worth is knowing deep in your core that you are enough exactly as you are. Not because of what you do for others. Not because of what you do for the company. Not because of your title. Not because of your performance or productivity. Just for existing as you.

Here are a few truths to remember: People pleasing is self-erasure. Rejection will not destroy you. Your worth is not contingent on being liked. Every ignored personal need is a signal that there is a missing boundary.

The Role of Boundaries in Business (and Life)

Great leaders know that saying yes to everything isn't a strength—it's a liability. What matters is not what you say yes to, but what you have the courage to say no to. And that's where boundaries come in; they act as a personal filter and keep out energy-draining distractions so that you can focus on what truly matters.

There are several types of boundaries worth mastering: emotional, physical, and energetic.

- **Emotional boundaries** are meant to protect your emotional well-being. These help you to not let others guilt, shame, or manipulate you. For example, refusing to take the blame for something you didn't do or declining to engage in a conversation with someone who is being passive-aggressive.
- **Physical boundaries** protect your body and reinforce your comfort. They reinforce your right to privacy and space. This could mean choosing not to hug a coworker if you feel uncomfortable or setting expectations about how close or far you would like people to be from your desk.
- **Energetic boundaries** are meant to protect your time and energy. They help prevent burnout by clarifying what you will and won't engage in—for instance, not taking after-hours calls, cutting down on overextended meetings, or pushing back against unreasonable demands.

You can apply the same approach to all of them, and it's very simple. Start with a clear "No." No qualifiers. No apologies. "No" is a complete sentence—a powerful one. You are a person with priorities. A professional with purpose. And saying "No" is your path to greater respect, clarity, and fulfillment. Every time you set a boundary, it's like sending yourself the message: I matter. I'm worthy. I can do this.

If you've been socialized to always be agreeable and accommodating, it may feel foreign or uncomfortable to assert your limits—especially if you are a woman in leadership. But here's the truth: Those who push back against your boundaries are doing so because they found some benefit in you not having any.

Work–Life Integration: Rethinking the Balance

Quite frankly, I'd like to retire the term "work-life balance." It implies that these two worlds are separate and in opposition, constantly tugging for control. But the truth is, you are not two separate people: a "professional self" and a "personal self." You bring your full identity into every room, whether that's in a team meeting or in your kitchen.

The goal is to find work that is meaningful, so instead of work–life balance, you create work–life integration. In other words, you don't want to slog through work you find unbearable just to reach your free time. You should want to enjoy the whole of your life, including the work that is part of it. That means not working in a toxic environment where being authentic, setting limits, or challenging norms is considered wrong. It also means not letting work consume your life. If your personal time is constantly interrupted by off-the-clock demands, that's not integration, that's being taken advantage of.

Work should be just *one* aspect of a fulfilling life. You are a human, not a robot, and you certainly weren't born to become one. If you find yourself lacking in joy, recovery, or connection outside of work, it's time to reassess.

Stephanie's Story: The Strength to Stop Overgiving

My colleague Stephanie embodies what I believe is the pinnacle of leadership: being both warm and firm at the same time. While working at the same company as me, I watched her develop from confusion and overcompensation to self-worth, self-esteem, and self-respect. Once she saw herself as valuable, there was no stopping her success.

> *Kids don't often say, "When I grow up, I want to work in human resources." In fact, many of my colleagues in HR fell into the profession rather than aspiring to it. Often, the profession finds us; we do not seek it out. I fell into HR shortly after moving*

to Santa Cruz, California, in the early 2000s. It was a temp job when the other options I had for work fell through. I thought I would work there for a few months while I looked for something better. But I quickly learned that HR was a good role for me. I have a tendency to want to take care of others (though that is to a fault at times). Early in my career, this manifested as taking the time to help employees fill out forms, understand leaves of absence, and review challenging situations in an effort to find workable solutions. This was all enough to propel me through my HR career, until it wasn't. What I didn't yet realize was how much I needed to learn about setting boundaries—not just with others, but with myself.

After seven years at my first HR job, I was laid off. During the meeting where I learned my fate, my manager said, "I don't think you are really cut out for HR anyway. You are too emotionally invested." While there was some truth to my level of emotional investment, this was coming from someone with an extremely cold stance; the HR director and owner saw employees as little more than incompetent cogs in the wheel and cut corners in every way they could. My first reaction was, "If I am gone, who is going to take care of the employees I support?" I genuinely cared for the individuals I helped in that restrictive environment. And, sure, my response was altruistic—but was it healthy when I was unexpectedly facing unemployment? Why was I so focused on taking care of others rather than first taking care of myself?

Honestly, I should have left that job years earlier. The environment was not right for me and I didn't know my worth. I thought it was my obligation to fix everything for others, even if it cost me my own mental health. I had no boundaries when it came to what people could take from me, and I was somewhat of a self-appointed savior. But what first seemed like a setback turned out to be a blessing. I learned a lot about HR and what I didn't want to do in the future. The next job I got was in a much healthier environment, guiding me on an upward trajectory that only continued ascending.

Many years later, I landed at a startup. In its early days, I met Andreas, thinking I had signed up for a two-month consulting job that would be "easy." That two-month gig became a job that lasted for five years and was anything but easy. I helped take the company from a startup with just a few people to nearly 100 employees and eventually earned the title of HR director. To quote Andreas, those early days felt like "building the airplane as it was taking off." Our fast pace prepared us to not only weather the standard startup difficulties, but also the insanity the world faced in 2020: the COVID-19 pandemic.

In March 2020, I was meeting with Andreas and the other members of the C-suite. Since I was the HR Director, they looked to me for recommendations on how to manage a possible office closure and shift to remote work as we all sheltered at home in an attempt to stay healthy. I looked around that group—knowing it was my job to oversee the well-being of employees—desperately seeking someone with more expertise than me. After all, my degrees are in English and Women's Studies. The extent of my knowledge on public health and pandemics stems from a fascination with apocalyptic literature and reading The Stand by Stephen King. I had no choice but to step up in the situation—and it went beyond the normal caregiving work I had been doing throughout my HR career. We had to navigate how to support employees as they transitioned to working from home while trying to keep themselves and their loved ones safe.

We got through those initial days, but the challenges did not stop. The workload was intense, getting normal tasks done as we got our product off the ground in the midst of global uncertainty. I was losing sleep over work, the stress of the pandemic, and the increasing sense of isolation. I was not taking good care of myself because I was pouring every bit of energy I had into taking care of employees who were scared and struggling. I found myself answering questions about COVID safety and other concerns way out of the scope of my expertise. In addition, we had to do a very emotional layoff as we eliminated certain roles followed by a period of high turnover that saw software engineers leaving for offers we could not possibly compete with.

I was sinking deeper into my job and losing touch with who I was as an individual. It was frustrating because I thought I was on the right path at my job. I had recently been promoted to HR director, which was a great step in my professional life. But brewing under the surface was the unhealthy path I was heading down. Because what happens when we do not see ourselves as worthy of the level of care we give to those we are leading? We disappear.

During that era of social distancing, I would often pop over to Andreas' house, which was close to where I lived at the time. This would usually start with a quick text saying, "You want to have fika?" Fika is a Swedish coffee break, but it is also the time when you socialize with your coworkers. We would end up hanging out in his backyard, sometimes with his family joining us. These meetings included socializing, but they also were a chance to talk through work issues and they became unofficial leadership coaching sessions. This quite possibly started one day when Andreas said, "Don't you realize that people see you as a leader? They listen to what you are saying and look to you for guidance." I was surprised because I certainly did not see myself that way, and I admitted, "I woke up one day and suddenly I was an HR leader. How did that happen?"

Maybe it was because I didn't see myself as a leader that I believed I didn't deserve the care I gave to others. In fact, I did not see myself as worthy of being a leader. Plus, that voice of my first manager in HR echoed in my head and made me believe that I was not good enough to be an HR leader. Andreas reminded me, "If most people see you as a leader and respect you, why are you listening to the very small number of voices that say otherwise?"

I was thankful for Andreas and other leaders at the company whose opinions, leadership styles, and advice I respected. In seeing that they felt the same about me, I began valuing my worth—not only as a leader, but a person. I was worthy of the care and compassion I was showing to others, especially during challenging times.

In 2022, I realized that my time at that company was drawing to a close. I could sense I was ready to move on and wanted to do so before I grew to resent the job and the amazing people I worked with. I also knew I needed a fresh start where I could leave behind lingering bad habits and take with me the good lessons I had learned during my time working with Andreas.

I landed a job that would require me to move from Orange County to Los Angeles, where I am originally from. As I packed up my apartment and chose what to take and what to toss, I figuratively packed the leadership habits I wanted to keep and left behind the ones I didn't. Into the dumpster they went, along with clothes that no longer fit, a broken chair long past its usefulness, and an old blanket held together by hope alone.

My first priority was to set clear boundaries between work and my personal life, which meant only responding to urgent messages outside of normal work hours. I had to shift my thinking to believe I deserved that time to myself—to do whatever I wanted, unrelated to work. Sometimes that's engaging in my volunteer work or being productive at home, and sometimes that's as simple as getting lost in a good book or enjoying a lazy Saturday morning in bed. Regardless of the activity, I stopped feeling guilty that I was not spending every waking hour in service to others. I decided that I was worth it. Just because someone else thought something was urgent didn't mean that thing was truly urgent.

My second priority was to no longer feel responsible for the things beyond my control. At my previous position, we sponsored a number of employees in the green card process. Of course waiting for immigration paperwork to come through was extremely stressful for the employees involved. For most of them, we were also sponsoring their family members, so that added an extra level of anxiety. I regularly had employees complaining about how much work it was and how slow things were moving. They were understandably worried about their status, but the reality is that I was doing all I could. I was at the mercy of the very burdensome system and backlogs that were beyond my control. Still, I felt guilty that we were not doing enough and it kept me up at night. But now, I was beginning to realize that there were simply limitations to what I could do for others.

While I was putting these priorities into practice at my new job, I also received more lessons outside of my HR job. I volunteer with the California Coalition for Women, which includes visiting women's prisons in California to meet with incarcerated people. We support them with advocacy work, prepare for parole hearings, and help address concerns they have. I have to set very clear boundaries in those relationships because I can't control how the prison is run—or whether we get responses to requests. And even when we do, I sometimes hit a policy wall. The more I have volunteered, the more I have realized to apply those same principles to my HR position.

I am proud to say, I am still volunteering in women's prisons and working as an HR leader at that same job (that I love) in Los Angeles. While I'm not completely free of the guilt that comes with saying no, I've come a long way from the people-pleaser who believed anything short of a full yes meant letting people down. Today if an employee is let down by a "no," it's okay. I give them space to feel their emotions and hopefully find another solution. I deeply care about people, but now it is not to a fault; I've turned my empathy into an asset rather than a hindrance.

More than anything, I am proud that I've arrived at a place where I feel confident in my abilities as a leader. Leadership does involve sacrifice, but it doesn't involve losing yourself. Leadership does involve removing barriers for employees, but it doesn't mean fixing everything for them. As leaders, we must set boundaries to take care of ourselves and our mental health, which then allows us to support others within our means. It requires knowing our limits, prioritizing self-care, and honoring the boundaries we set. If we don't, it sends the message that self-care is not important and that the job is above all else in our lives.

If we are going to build healthy communities, it starts with leaders taking care of themselves. Even though we aren't in the pandemic anymore, we are still leading through challenging times and economic uncertainty. My organization just recently faced a closure that lasted nearly a month due to the Los Angeles fires in January 2025. Employees were without power or had to evacuate. In times like these, it becomes even more important that we make the space to take care of ourselves in order to be respected as leaders and, more importantly, to respect ourselves as leaders.

The CEO of my organization held a virtual town hall about a week after the fires broke out. She reminded us that the highest priority was individual stability. Until we had individual stability, we could not focus on organizational stability, and until we had organizational stability, we could not help the larger community. She said, "If at any point you lose individual stability, you go back to square one." This was boundary-setting at its finest, and she was modeling it for all of us. It also put me in a position to be a better leader through the crisis because I did first focus on myself and get through those initial days of the fires when I was without power and close to evacuating.

And when I reached individual stability, I was able to not only support those in my organization, but truly be present with them. And I've come to realize that is the most important thing of all. Sometimes what we need from leaders is just that: presence. People don't always want advice or solutions—sometimes, they just want to be seen and heard.

As Stephanie's story shows, boundary-setting is a skill that takes time. It's not a one-and-done fix. It's a daily practice. One clear no at a time. One conscious decision to honor your values. One moment of choosing peace over someone else's approval. Like any leadership skill, it strengthens with intention and repetition.

Activities for Setting Boundaries and Commanding Respect

Boundaries will lead you to higher levels of self-respect. They also provide the initial stepping stones for you to connect with your highest value, purpose, and potential (which we'll dive deeper into in Section IV: Purpose & Transformation). Since boundaries won't set themselves, complete these activities before moving on to the next chapter.

#1: Start Small:

Say "no" once this week. (Or an alternative to no, such as "I can't make it." or "I'm unavailable at that time.") Just once. Say no to a meeting, a task, or even a social event—and don't feel like you have to give a reason why. Be okay with the silence that might follow afterward. The more you do this, the more comfortable and confident you will get.

#2: Make Daily Promises to Yourself:

Some people struggle to keep promises to others, but many more people struggle to keep promises to themselves. Pay attention to this and know it's time to level up with this simple task: each morning for the next week make *one* personal promise—something tangible that you'll follow through on. This is where true integrity begins: keeping your word to yourself.

#3: Take a Deeper Dive:

If you recognize that you need more support in this area, pause here and work through my free guided journaling ebook, *90 Days to Self-Worth*. It's a structured tool designed to help rewire your internal narrative. You can find it at the QR code at the end of this chapter.

#4. Tier Your Yeses:

Not every request deserves your time. Create levels of access:

- Tier One: Your inner circle (five people) who get your "yes" without question.
- Tier Two: Trusted connections (ten people) who you say yes to when it aligns with your goals.
- Tier Three: Everyone else—default to "no" unless it's truly aligned.

This isn't harsh—it's smart. You are not a public resource.

#5: Fire People from Your Life:

You don't need permission to exercise personal power in your life, and it's time to start using it. Some people simply don't deserve a seat at your table. Remember how we just "tiered our yeses"? Here's a pro tip: Drama enthusiasts, gossipers, and energy vampires go straight to Tier 4—where they get none of your time or energy. Ever. (You're welcome!)
Of course, this can be especially tough for women who've been conditioned to caretake and keep the peace. And to be clear, we're not talking about firing your children or elderly parents. This is about distancing yourself from adults who consistently drain you. If cutting ties feels daunting, start small. Reduce how much access they have, delay your responses, and give yourself permission to protect your energy. Know that they will do what they can to drag you back into their never-ending story. Don't let them. You don't need to know what happens next in their soap opera.

Call to Action for Leaders

As you've learned by now, leadership is about so much more than hitting your numbers. Your employees' self-development.

The type of culture you foster. Boundaries in the workplace. These are all vital to the success of your organization. Make sure you are doing the following.

#1: Know the Boundaries:

You can't support your employees if you're not familiar with the many kinds of boundaries that exist: time boundaries, mental boundaries, physical boundaries, material boundaries, conversational boundaries, etc. Spend some time reading about different types of boundaries to educate yourself. This will not only help you and your employees, but the work culture as a whole.

#2: Model What You Preach:

If you want your team to respect boundaries, you must first demonstrate that you respect your own. That means don't send emails at midnight. Use your PTO—and encourage others to do the same. Decline meetings that lack a goal or purpose. Block time for deep work and strategy—and honor it. Boundaries set from the top establish cultural norms and create healthier power dynamics.

#3: Equip Your Team With Language:

Language shapes behavior—and behavior shapes culture… Teach your employees and other leaders to communicate with strength and clarity. Offer short workshops or conversations on topics like "How to say no effectively," "How to set clear expectations," or "How to self-advocate without guilt." Empowered communication leads to empowered employees.

#4: Set Clear Expectations While Offering Flexibility:

People thrive when they have freedom within structure. So, define clear deadlines and priorities while also allowing for things like adjustable schedules, remote work, or individual needs.

#5: Utilize Accountability:

Help yourself, other leaders, and employees by structuring more accountability into the organization. This might include mandatory discussions around boundaries during one-on-one performance reviews or new boundary-focused organizational policies.

Scan this QR code to check out more resources.

Chapter 8: Building Your Strategic Network

"Networking is not about just connecting people. It's about connecting people with people, people with ideas, and people with opportunities."
— *Michele Jennae*

A strategic network is more than a LinkedIn contact list or a stack of business cards from industry events. Think of your network like your tribe. It's a true ecosystem of relationships, among individuals, businesses, and organizations, built intentionally to support your goals, challenge your thinking, and expand your access to opportunities. The best networks don't just add value—they multiply it, by helping you stay competitive, informed, and resilient in an ever-changing professional landscape.

If your goal is to accelerate your career trajectory, a strategic network is one of the most powerful tools at your disposal. In this chapter, we'll break down what a business network truly is, why it's essential, who should be part of it, and how to build one with intention. Your options range from creating your own to leaning into peer groups to engaging more with people in your company. We'll also explore how women—especially those in male-dominated industries—can approach networking with both strategic rigor and authenticity to foster long-term professional fulfillment. My colleague Cindy is an expert on network creation, so we'll hear her story and wisdom as well.

Constructing Your Network Purposefully

Before building your network, it's critical to understand what practices are effective and what practices are ineffective, so let's go over some rules.

Rule #1: Don't treat networks as transactional tools.

Prioritize building genuine human connections. Offer help to others, and be open to receiving it in return. Networking thrives on reciprocity, not opportunism.

Rule #2: Build your network proactively.

The most successful professionals know that the time to build relationships is *before* you need them. That way, when opportunity arises—or a crisis strikes—you have a powerful team behind you.

Rule #3: Surround yourself with people who are ahead of you.

A strong network should stretch your thinking and, at times, feel slightly intimidating. If everyone in your circle mirrors your experience or stage of career, it may be time to reach higher. In other words, don't "settle" into—or for—a network.

Rule #4: Give back.

Offer support to peers and to those who are newer to your company or industry. This is a key way to see your leadership worth.

Rule #5: Ensure you have objective voices in your corner.

While a supervisor may serve as a strong sponsor, they should not double as your mentor. The best mentors are those who don't have direct influence over your performance and advancement (such as a leader from another division, a former manager, or a respected professional outside of your organization). Why? Because they are free from the politics of your workplace and not worried about competing with you, which allows them to be honest, supportive, and free of hidden agendas.

Rule #6: Don't wait for permission to pursue these relationships.

One critical disparity I've observed: Men, more often, actively *seek* mentorship, while women often wait for mentorship to be *offered*. (Don't wait. It's not coming!) Your growth is too important to leave in someone else's hands. Take action now—make it known that you're seeking to build your network. (If you don't know where to get started, the Power Without Permission community can help. Learn more at the QR code at the end of this chapter.)

Far too often, I see women initiate networking efforts only after encountering career stagnation or when urgently needing a new job. And, when they do, they tend to limit outreach to peers or those in familiar roles, avoiding individuals in positions of greater influence. This approach breaks many of the rules I just mentioned. It is transactional, reactive, and—let's be honest—safe. At the same time, I understand that many women already carry a massive mental, emotional, and logistical load in both their personal and professional lives. So the idea of "putting yourself out there" for one more thing can feel like too much. But here's the hard truth: You can't afford not to. Research shows that roughly 70% of jobs are never shared on job sites, and nearly 80% are filled through either personal or professional connections (Bradshaw, 2025). More than anything, these stats show that *who you know* is vital to your success. That doesn't mean you need to hustle harder or fill every hour of your schedule; it means being intentional with the time and energy you do have.

Another thing to keep in mind when constructing your network is who should be a part of it. The quick answer: Your network should be vast and diverse. It should include individuals who encourage your growth, "A" players who are further along than you, those who bring out your best, and people you can support and mentor in return. These roles can take the form of mentors, sponsors, advisors, allies, collaborators, and mentees.

Advisors, Coaches, Mentors, and Sponsors

While these four roles contribute differently, they share a common purpose: advancing your personal and professional development. I've sought out many of these relationships myself—even at the height of my career—because I knew that growth doesn't stop when you reach the top. What I can tell you honestly is that working with advisors, coaches, mentors, and sponsors is like condensing a thousand years of experience into your own career. Why? Because they offer you compounded knowledge, saving you years of struggle and catapulting you years into the future.

Let's take a closer look at the role of each one:

Advisors: Your subject-matter experts. They offer targeted insight and direction in a specific area of expertise. Their guidance is often direct, focused, and short-term. For example, you might work with an advisor when you are looking to expand into a new market.

Coaches: Your performance consultant. They work with you in a structured and goal-oriented way to help you enhance your capabilities, overcome barriers, and maximize your potential. For example, you might hire a coach when you want to improve your leadership presence.

Mentors: Your long-term sages. They share insight, offer feedback, and help you navigate challenges. These relationships are often informal, built on trust, designed to last long-term, and meant to foster growth across multiple dimensions—professional, personal, and leadership. According to a recent survey by CNBC, from working adults who reported having a mentor, 90% stated that they were satisfied with their jobs and salaries (Smith, 2024). Satisfaction was significantly lower with those who reported not having mentors. You might seek out a mentor when you are navigating a career transition and you want insight from someone who walked a similar path and whose core values match yours.

Sponsors: Your advocates. While they may offer guidance, their primary role is to champion your visibility and advancement—especially when you're not in the room, which is often when it matters most. They will use their influence to open doors, create opportunities, and position you for elevation. For instance, you might need a sponsor when you are aiming to get a promotion.

Allyship, Alliances, and Peer Groups

Success rarely happens in isolation. In high-performing environments, collaboration—not competition—is what drives change and deepens impact. Hence where allyship, alliances, and peer groups come in.

Allyship is rooted in advocacy. It involves challenging biases, supporting others, and promoting equity—especially in spaces where access to power isn't equal. Effective allies act with empathy and curiosity, and have the courage to speak up, even when it's uncomfortable. This might look like men advocating for women or senior leaders sponsoring emerging talent.

Alliances are collaborative and intentional partnerships built around mutual goals. They can be built between individuals or can be cross-departmental, cross-functional, or cross-industry, and can range from informal social bonds to formal strategic partnerships. While they might not tackle systemic issues, they create shared meaningful outcomes, such as gaining market share or tackling a larger project together.

Peer Groups offer an invaluable space for growth and reflection among professionals at similar stages of their careers. These cohorts hold frequent meetings and provide emotional support, diverse perspectives, and accountability—both in your work and your personal life, because a thriving personal life fuels professional excellence.

Navigating Male-Dominated Industries

Let's be candid—this isn't always easy. Carving out space in male-dominated industries requires equal parts strategic acumen and emotional intelligence.

Women in these fields often have to expend extra effort to be heard, included, respected, and promoted. Thus, they naturally gravitate toward the few other women who are present. There's no doubt that women's circles are essential in these spaces for support and connection. However, meaningful transformation can only happen in *integrated* spaces—where women and men work together to reshape culture.

Thus, you must step confidently into male-dominated rooms—and bring another woman with you whenever possible. And remember: There is no need to mimic the men around you. Be strategic and adaptable, while leading from a warm yet firm feminine power.

- Speak with authority.
- Lead with data.
- Be ready to shift your strategy. (But never shift your values!)
- Identify a few men who will vouch for you and create space for you.
- Learn to balance ethos (credibility), pathos (emotion), and logos (logic).

Cindy's Story: Building Her Village from the Ground Up

One of my colleagues, Cindy, navigates a male-dominated space daily and consistently rises by leveraging her network and showing up with strong confidence and clear communication. Her story can inspire anyone.

> *In high school, I served as president of the Associated Student Body (ASB) all four years. The main reason I joined ASB was that my dad was overprotective. My siblings and I weren't allowed to hang out with friends after school or on weekends, and I had seen him give my sister a hard time about staying after school for dances and activities. If something was considered "official school business,"*

he was more likely to allow it, so I learned from her experience by joining ASB. What started as a practical solution became something much bigger. While I wasn't part of the popular crowd, I naturally connected with people from all different circles and found myself floating between different friend groups. I enjoyed knowing everyone's names, organizing solutions, and helping things run smoothly.

But life shifted dramatically at the start of my senior year, right after I submitted my college applications. My father suffered a sudden heart attack in the middle of the night. My mother discovered him unconscious and unable to control his body. In a state of distress, she banged on my bedroom door. I saw him on the floor and immediately called 911. Following the operator's instructions, I attempted CPR as my younger brother—only seven at the time and too young to grasp the gravity of the situation—laughed, thinking my dad was playing a joke on us. Shortly after, the paramedics arrived and transported him to the hospital while I, newly licensed to drive, followed closely behind. That drive felt endless and unreal as I tried to stay hopeful, unable to fully process what was happening.

Devastatingly, en route to the hospital, he flatlined. And his sudden death didn't just take him away—it took me away too. I had only applied to colleges locally, planning to stay close to home, so it was a shock when my mom decided to return to Taiwan with my younger brother that summer before I started at UC Irvine. My older sister and I were left to pack up our childhood home alone. I learned what isolation and abandonment felt like for the first time.

ANDREAS PETTERSSON

College should have been a fresh start, but I was a mess, emotionally and physically. The girl who had naturally drawn people in suddenly wanted nothing to do with anyone. While other freshmen embraced new experiences and built connections, I clung to familiar faces and old relationships. I joined Associated Students of UC Irvine (ASUCI), but only because it felt familiar after my ASB experience in high school. Beyond that, I avoided putting myself out there with new people. The curious, social person I'd always been was suddenly a stranger. Those years of loss taught me resilience in ways I didn't recognize at the time. Having to handle my father's death, manage family responsibilities alone, and rebuild my sense of self while grieving quietly built the problem-solving skills and emotional strength I would later draw on as a leader. I learned to function under extreme pressure, to make difficult decisions when others couldn't, and to keep moving forward by compartmentalizing my emotions and focusing on what needed to be done. I also learned that my ability to build authentic relationships wasn't just a personality trait—it was my superpower. And trauma had temporarily severed me from myself and that core strength.

My reconnection to myself began in unexpected places. I took a job at The Cheesecake Factory because I needed something that was demanding enough that my mind wouldn't wander to everything I'd lost. The restaurant environment turned out to be exactly what I needed—it reconnected me to the energy I thrived in during high school: fast-paced, dynamic, and deeply people-oriented. During busy shifts, I didn't have the mental space to dwell on grief. Gradually, I started to notice that the work felt familiar: reading customers quickly, managing multiple priorities, bringing energy to chaotic situations. Pieces of who I used to be were quietly re-emerging.

I got into wedding planning for similar reasons. I needed something to occupy my time on the weekends when the campus was empty. UC Irvine was a commuter school, and I needed to fill the void. The industry was demanding, with long hours and intense weekend events. It was hands-on, creative, and filled with high-energy problem-solving. I ended up working for a couple of wedding and event planning companies, even considering starting my own at one point—but the sustainability of owning a business made me abandon the idea.

After graduating in 2010, I was at a standstill with the professional path I wanted to take. Job hunting was brutal. It was one of the worst job markets in history: the Great Recession. Unemployment was near 10%, millions of jobs had been lost, and I spent two years getting nowhere, despite applying everywhere. I had no industry network to rely on and no mentor to guide me. At my lowest point, I told my mom, "If someone would just give me a chance, I would work so hard." I meant it. I was ready to prove myself—I just needed someone to open the door.

Eventually, I reached out to a former colleague from the wedding industry who had transitioned into a corporate role. She informed me there was a front desk position open at her company. "It's not glamorous," she said, "but you will have a chance to grow from there." I applied, and when I got the offer, I took it immediately. Finally, someone was giving me that chance.

What I didn't realize was how perfectly positioned that front desk job would make me. I got to meet everyone who came through the lobby, learned about different departments, and got exposed to the corporate world. More importantly, people all over the company got to see me in action. Within a few months, when someone in education services went on maternity leave, I was promoted to backfill her role. But when she returned, I found myself without a defined role once again. Then came the real shock: the CEO asked me to join his new startup as the first employee. Here I thought he barely knew my name, let alone that he'd want me on his team.

Looking back, I can see what happened. When opportunities presented themselves, I always said yes, without hesitation—even when I had no idea what I was getting into. He saw my courage and competitive drive before I saw it in myself.

At his startup, I wore every hat imaginable. I helped the company from the ground up, scaling the team to over twenty-five people while building foundational processes. Eventually, I transitioned into a customer success role, but soon realized I wanted something different. My conversations with customers sparked ideas. I saw patterns in their feedback, gaps in what we were offering, and opportunities we were missing.

Eventually, I approached our CTO, product manager, and UX designer with a concept that could bridge a gap in our product. The CTO's response changed everything: "This is the right stuff. Cindy, you're thinking like a product person, in a way that shows you understand how all the pieces fit together." I had no idea that's what I was doing—I was just trying to solve problems I heard every day.

At some point, our product manager left the company, and the CTO suggested I consider transitioning into product management. The idea terrified and excited me. I had no formal training, but I'd been observing, learning, and apparently thinking like a product person without realizing it—so I said yes.

Though I had a natural eye for design, a sense for how products should function, and a deep understanding of customer needs, the learning curve was steep. The first few weeks, I'd go home completely fried, feeling like my brain had run a marathon. But I also felt more energized than I had in years. I was solving puzzles I'd never encountered before, and every day brought something new to figure out.

Our CTO became my mentor. When I felt overwhelmed by technical discussions, he translated complex concepts in ways I could grasp. Once, when I told him I felt like I was drowning, he said something that stuck with me: "Welcome to product management. You'll never get it all done. It's all about good choices and solid triage." He empathized with my overwhelm but was confident I'd push through it. I also learned from him that the best managers make you famous. He continuously highlighted my contributions and made sure my work was visible to leadership. What I appreciated most was his authenticity as a leader, which gave me permission to be myself too.

Unfortunately, when our startup culture started falling apart under poor leadership, he left for a larger software company. (What sold him on the new role was meeting Andreas, the CEO.) Since we'd worked well together and I'd expressed interest in joining him, he reached out as soon as they had an opening. I got the job—and learned the difference between having relationships and actually leaning on them when it mattered.

ANDREAS PETTERSSON

It didn't take long for Andreas to become both my mentor and sponsor. His superpower is seeing more in people than they see in themselves, and he acts on it. He continuously gave me opportunities that stretched me—like managing complex, high-stakes business relationships with other companies. These were strategically important deals that had real commercial impact, where failure could have reflected poorly on him as CEO. That level of trust was transformative.

The biggest gift he gave me was recommending me for SHE Counsel. I wasn't seeking out women's leadership networks. Honestly, I didn't even know they existed. But Andreas saw that my natural way of connecting with people could be even more powerful when surrounded by other women navigating similar leadership challenges.

Being part of this group helped me shed my impostor syndrome in a way I hadn't expected. I realized it didn't matter what stage of your career or what industry you're in—the challenges are remarkably similar. More importantly, I saw that I'd experienced more than I gave myself credit for. This newfound confidence gave me the voice to speak up and ask for a seat at our quarterly EOS planning sessions, even as the youngest member of the leadership team. Looking back, I see a pattern I couldn't recognize while living it: losing my father and having to grow up fast forged a resilience that allowed me to function under pressure, make decisions when others couldn't, and keep moving forward. More than that, it taught me to value the people who lift you up when you can't lift yourself.

I was fortunate to work with mentors and sponsors who genuinely wanted to see me succeed, and today I've become that same kind of leader. I look for opportunities to lift up people who remind me of myself—talented, but not yet seeing their own potential. Whether it's someone just starting in Product Management who feels overwhelmed, or someone who needs encouragement to take on a challenge that feels too big, I try to be that person for them.

The most powerful thing I've learned is this: Executive networks aren't built through strategic networking—they're built through authentic connections with people who see something in you. The key is being ready to say yes when they offer to help. And when you can, continue the cycle by lifting others. You never know what kind of lasting impact you might have on someone's journey.

Just like Cindy, your network (your tribe) can become your edge. If you don't have one yet, don't worry—neither did she, and now she's surrounded by people who would pick up the phone for her any time. Why? Because she has spent that time investing in her network and is the type of person who will follow through.

Activities for Building Your Strategic Network

I'm not exaggerating when I tell you that most of my career success comes from my network. This isn't about small talk or collecting business cards. It's about constructing a foundation that sustains your long-term growth—professionally and personally. So, approach it with boldness and intentionality. Your future self—and your future success—will thank you.

You know what comes next: Try these activities and don't move on to the next chapter until you've done them.

#1: Build Your Personal Board of Directors:

This isn't about collecting titles—it's about assembling wisdom. Build a diverse group of people who provide insight, accountability, and support across different areas of your life. Include colleagues, mentors, industry leaders, and even people outside your field who broaden your view.

#2: Say Yes:

Just as Cindy mentioned, it's so important to say yes when others offer you help or give you an opportunity. You might not think you deserve the help or are ready for the opportunity, but maybe the people in your tribe know you're worth it. Don't self-sabotage—say yes. You are brilliant. You are ready. Just do it.

#3: Attend a Networking Event This Month:

Commit to a local professional gathering—be it a conference, workshop, or roundtable. Make sure to not just show up, but show up with purpose and intention. Introduce yourself. Follow up with those you meet. That's how relationships begin.

#4: Get Out of Your People Comfort Zone:

Do not only talk to people who you are comfortable with. Approach the people who challenge you or make you feel out of your depth. There is a lesson to be learned or an opportunity to be had by engaging with people who are much different from you—and you might just be surprised by what comes out of those interactions!

#5: Get Involved in Your Community:

You never know who you are meant to meet, and it won't only be people in your company or industry. Volunteer locally. Go to a fun craft workshop. Join a local group or board.

A Call to Action for Leaders

Jeff Weber, a former Forbes Council member, shared that a survey by his company "found that 77% of employees feel they are on their own to determine their career development" (2019).

This signals a significant gap in leadership—and a clear opportunity for you to step in and guide career growth.

As a leader, one of the most powerful investments you can make is empowering your people to build their networks. When employees grow, so does your organization. (The opposite is also true. You're welcome!) New relationships bring new insights, more opportunities, and fresh energy. The return on investment is exponential. Make sure you are doing the following.

#1: Foster Cross-Functional Collaboration:

Encourage departments to break down silos by hosting intentional events around shared projects or industry trends. This creates an opportunity for employees at all levels to connect with leaders and peers.

#2: Provide Resources:

Offer coaching, mentoring, and development programs at all levels of the organizations. Pair emerging talent (mentees) with experienced professionals (mentors) and have them both take training courses, that way *everyone* is leveling up.

#3: Be a Mentor and Sponsor Yourself:

Don't only offer up other experienced professionals' time; offer up your own. Even if you can't take on many, know that just one makes a difference. Sponsor or mentor an emerging leader.

#4: Spot the Talent:

Remember how, in my personal story, I shared that when I was in my early thirties, an executive recognized my potential and put me into a leadership program? I went on to do the same for others—you should too.

#5: Allow Employees to Join Peer Groups:

Remember how Cindy joined the SHE Counsel? And how helpful she mentioned it has been for her? Support your employees—especially women—by encouraging participation in peer groups inside and outside your organization. These groups can build confidence, broaden perspectives, and deepen connections.

Scan this QR code to check out more resources.

Chapter 9: Taking Action

"The future depends on what you do today." — Mahatma Gandhi

If you've made it this far into the book, it's clear you understand that self-awareness, mindset, and intention are essential for growth as a businesswoman. However, awareness alone is not transformation. Reading about growth isn't growth. Talking about leadership isn't leadership. You cannot merely think your way to the next level—you must act your way there. It is only through consistent, deliberate action that your ambitions become your achievements.

So if aspects of your life feel misaligned—whether it's a toxic work environment, an underperforming team, inadequate compensation, or lack of clarity around your goals—it's time to act. Resign from the job. Negotiate the raise. Set the boundary. Open the door, and walk through it. You don't need permission.

A reliable way to see if you're already taking meaningful action in your life is by asking yourself this question: When people have given you advice or tools recently, have you used them or ignored them? For example, have you been doing the targeted activities at the end of each chapter of this book? If you've been completing them, you're already in motion. (Phenomenal job!) If you've been bypassing them, you're neglecting your progress and potential.

Listen, you didn't invest time into this book to stay the same. And I certainly didn't write it to keep you comfortable. This is your imperative wake-up call. If you're waiting for the "perfect" time or telling yourself you don't need certain activities, know this: That mindset will keep you stuck. Because if you only *absorb* information and don't *apply* it, nothing will change. And the cost of inaction is steep: The promotion won't come, the boundaries won't hold, and the confidence you crave won't be developed.

Thus, in this chapter, we're going to confront what truly separates you from the life you envision: procrastination, risk aversion, and the tendency to linger indefinitely in the ideation stage. We'll also learn from my colleague Marlene, a woman who exemplifies the power of bold execution. She doesn't just talk about change, she embodies it. Her journey is motivating for anyone ready to say, "Enough learning. I'm all in."

Procrastination: The Silent Saboteur

Procrastination is the quiet destroyer of potential. It cloaks itself in rationalizations like "I need more clarity," "It's not the right time," or "I'm not ready yet." It immobilizes you in a cycle of thought, delaying tangible progress despite constant mental preoccupation with change. It leaves you stuck and frustrated because you *want* to do projects more efficiently; you *want* to be on time to meetings; you *want* to uplevel your life. Yet, your reality doesn't reflect your intentions.

Nearly everyone struggles with procrastination at some point, with 95% of people admitting to engaging in it occasionally. However, 20% of adults identify as chronic procrastinators (Banks, 2020). Left unchecked, this bad habit can erode careers, self-confidence, mental and physical health, and life goals.

The reason procrastination is so pervasive is that taking action and forming new habits inherently involves discomfort. The fear of failure, the fear of uncertainty, and the pressure of perfectionism—these things will all arise. In some cases, one's procrastination is rooted in something more complex, such as neurodivergent conditions like ADHD, anxiety, or OCD, which require professional support. (If you are in this camp, don't bypass seeking help. If someone has poor vision, they acquire glasses, right? Treat nonphysical traits the same way you treat physical ones.) *But* for the vast majority of us, procrastination is not tied to something deeper and it is simply a behavioral response to perceived discomfort. And most people prefer to avoid discomfort, even if it means staying unhappy and stagnant. However, comfort is rarely the path to excellence.

From Idea to Execution

So what does the path to excellence entail? Well, it does involve those ideas that we procrastinate on. Many professionals are *rich* in ideas: vision boards, strategic plans, business names, coaching programs, service offerings. But ideas are just that—ideas. Ideation without execution is simply living in illusion. (Stop getting high on the idea of it. You're welcome!) If you want to be a doer instead of a dreamer, execute consistently.

Execution is one of the most critical skills I've observed in senior leaders. They don't endlessly deliberate; they take action. And that is how you overcome procrastination: by developing a bias toward action. That means making decisions without all the information, taking a step without a guaranteed outcome, and being okay with messy forward motion.

Now, don't go crazy and start executing everything at once. You don't have to overhaul your entire life in one day. You simply need to take the next step. Just start! One small action is all it takes. *One*. Small, manageable moves—often referred to as microactions—compound into transformation. One email. One phone call. One difficult conversation. One calculated risk. Executed consistently, microactions will outperform massive half-executed plans every time.

Here are five practical execution strategies:

#1: Set attainable goals:

For instance, if your aim is to read more, don't set yourself up for failure by committing to an entire book in one day. Aim for 10 pages or one chapter per day. Progress is what matters—it gives you experience and reveals things you wouldn't otherwise see.

#2: Focus on High-Impact Tasks:

People often fill their calendars to feel valuable, but busyness doesn't always equal productivity or impact. Ask yourself: Are you doing what matters, or just doing? Identify the top one to three actions that will move you closer to your goals, then commit to completing those before anything else. (Pro tip: choose a 30-minute window each week on the same day—such as every Friday—to reflect and plan your priorities for the week ahead. Leaders do this and don't compromise.)

#3: Leverage Your Support System:

Delegating or asking for assistance is not a weakness, but a necessary leadership skill. High-functioning teams and successful leaders know how to allocate resources and tasks effectively. This frees up more of your time so you can maximize your value and output.

#4: Allow for Recovery Time:

Sustainable productivity requires rest. Avoid burnout by integrating time management tools like the Pomodoro Method: 25 minutes of focus, followed by 5minutes of rest, or 50 minutes of focus followed by 10 minutes of rest.

#5: Reflect:

There is a great book and concept called *Ready, Fire, Aim* by Michael Masterson. I highly recommend reading it for the full depth and insight offered in the book, but for now, I'll share why I love the title and concept. Most people spend their lives aiming for things, but they're never truly ready and rarely, if ever, fire. (By "fire," I mean take action). It's time to level up. Stop aiming and fire. If you find out that it wasn't aligned, aim somewhere new and fire again. So let me ask you: Are you aiming but never firing? Or are you ready? Do you take action: fire, aim, fire, aim, fire, aim?

Intentional planning, clear communication, and consistent follow-through—this is your new standard if you want your vision boards, strategic plans, business names, or coaching programs to become a reality. This is what is required for sustainable growth. There's no magic formula—you just have to do the work.

The Power of Taking Calculated Risks

When we execute, *how* we do it matters—taking action doesn't mean acting impulsively. To bring back the aiming and firing concept: You don't want to fire in every direction. You'll learn nothing that way. You want your arrows to go into the same general area, and pivot later if need be. That's calculated risk-taking, and it requires balance. Courage and care. Intuition and data. You don't want to leap off a cliff blindly; you want to jump with a parachute.

For example, if you come to realize that your current work environment isn't bringing out your best, you wouldn't want to just take the first job offer you get in a new city to hurry out of the position you've come to despise. You would want to assess the potential benefits against the risks—new places and new opportunities weighed against unfamiliarity and relocation costs.

Thus, calculated risks are best made from a place of emotional regulation and self-awareness. One tool I use with clients is the concept of leadership keys. Think of it this way: You wouldn't hand someone the keys to a vehicle if they were in a heightened emotional state and frantic. The same applies to decision-making. If your nervous system is dysregulated, your judgment will be compromised. In such moments, pause. Take away your leadership keys so you don't get into a wreck. Reclaim your calm. This is an important part of your personal evolution—recognizing when it's necessary to hand your leadership keys to a trusted advisor, coach, or peer.

Not every calculated risk will yield results or perfect outcomes—but that's not the objective. The objective is to evolve, to stretch yourself, and expand your range of what's possible. That's how you get clarity. Just remember: Concentrated efforts yield concentrated results.

Marlene's Story: Born to Move Forward

Over the span of six months of leadership coaching, Marlene evolved exponentially. And I can say with confidence that her success was due to taking consistent, fearless action. Her introspection, humility, and bold decision-making make her an expert on this topic—traits every leader should aspire to cultivate.

In January 1963, in the tense aftermath of the Cuban Missile Crisis, my Cuban parents made the life-altering decision to flee Havana for Miami. Only weeks later, they discovered they were expecting me. Although they briefly considered ending the pregnancy, they ultimately chose to continue—another act of courage that shaped my existence. I was born on October 9 of that year, into a world already marked by their brave choices—a legacy that would later shape my own instinct to act when it mattered most.

However, their decision to seek freedom did come at a cost. We struggled, sometimes enduring long stretches of hardship, as many Cuban refugees did. Plus, our family was permanently cut off from the homeland they loved, never again able to return to see parents, siblings, or elders. This displacement bred a kind of intergenerational grief that lingered quietly beneath the surface of my childhood—a constant emotional undercurrent of longing, worry, and unspoken loss. I existed in a world of unseen burdens, constantly analyzing, sensing, and surviving, which drew me toward the unseen forces that shape our lives—emotions, trauma, and social norms.

By the time I turned eighteen, I felt a strong yearning for personal and spiritual reinvention. I left my family and hometown for Washington, D.C. in 1983, with nothing more than determination and two cardboard boxes full of ambition. I had no financial safety net, so I hustled with heart in both work and school. I earned a B.A. in Political Science from The George Washington University and went on to complete an M.S. in Broadcast Journalism from Columbia University.

Over the decades, I built a dynamic career, rising from production associate to producer to director of programming. Eventually, I earned my way into my current role as Vice President of Public Programs at a prestigious Cultural Center. I've worked with luminaries, like Steve Jobs and Hillary Clinton, and renowned organizations, like ABC News and The History Channel. What makes it special is that none of it came easily or was handed to me; I simply had vision and grit. Every milestone was earned through my unwavering commitment to move forward–traits deeply ingrained in me as the daughter of immigrants and a product of my lineage's life of resilience.

However, despite my outward achievements, I reached a point where my inner world felt painfully misaligned. I realized I had been living under the unconscious control of my younger self–a child filled with rage, sadness, and a deep-rooted need to please. Why did I need to be a "good girl" when I was a mature, respected, successful woman? I knew I wasn't alone–this was the ultimate female curse. My internal dissonance was a byproduct of the gendered expectations–familial, societal, cultural, emotional, physical, universal–most women are conditioned to uphold. We are all taught to be "good girls" from the moment we can speak. In exchange, we receive rewards and approval–from parents, teachers, and employers. But the price we pay is often self-abandonment. In other words: If a woman is not pretty, quiet, and compliant... what is she? We can't simply exist.

While this knowledge had been slowly simmering in me for years, it all erupted to the surface after the passing of my mother. There was a total breakdown among the remaining family members. So much revolutionary and intergenerational trauma remained unresolved. Cuba had endured multiple revolutions in 60 years, which came with constant chaos, terror, and bloodshed that lived on in us. My mother's life had been filled with that suffering and, for years, I had unknowingly been mirroring her same patterns. If I remained the same, I would follow in her footsteps. So I made the bold decision to forge an even newer path, beyond the path I'd forged when I left home for college in 1983. I vowed to confront my pain, heal, and redefine my life.

The process was neither simple nor painless. It meant having difficult, vulnerable conversations with my siblings. It also meant standing in my power and making unpopular decisions—like firing an arrogant, insolent male colleague, an act that challenged the machista cultural norms I'd been taught to respect. It meant allowing myself to feel emotions I'd suppressed for decades. In this context, taking action meant stepping into discomfort again and again.

I vividly recall the first time I said "no" with conviction: to a lousy boyfriend, when I kicked him out of my San Francisco apartment. I was terrified—of what he might think or what lie on the other side of that decision. But I knew I had to go through with it and stood my ground. And each subsequent act of self-respect built on the last. Just as professional success breeds more success, personal empowerment breeds more empowerment.

One of the most insidious myths is that staying where you are is easier. In truth, remaining stuck—mentally, emotionally, spiritually—is far more painful than taking the risk to change. And yet, many people remain stagnant, clinging to their excuses until the pain of not evolving outweighs the fear of growth. So, if you are stuck, remember that the teacher—whether a coach, a book, or a divine nudge—appears only when the student is ready and willing.

For me, that readiness and willingness is anchored in remembering where I came from. I am alive today because my parents made the courageous decision not to end my life. I have the life I have because my parents made the courageous decision to flee tyranny and oppression in search of something better. I am a vessel carrying the legacy of those silenced in Cuba, and it's my responsibility to live with radical agency. To stop wasting time in situations—or with people—that don't align with my soul's truth. To claim my power and break free from limiting narratives. To question the status quo and take initiative because the future is unwritten.

Taking action is not just about professional advancement; it's also about honoring your life, your lineage, and your highest potential. It's about making space for a world where future generations of women are freer, braver, and bolder. So, if I don't take action, I am not doing my part to dismantle the systems that confine us or fulfilling my sacred obligation to become the fullest expression of myself.

I have worked too hard and overcome too much to betray myself now. Likewise, you have worked too hard and overcome too much to betray yourself. Take the actions you need to take—you owe it to the person you were, the person you are, and the person you're becoming.

Activities for Taking Action

As Marlene's story shows, the traits necessary for growth are curiosity, humility, and the willingness to act—even in the face of discomfort or uncertainty. Now it's your turn. No more thinking—just doing. The activities below are microactions—small, strategic steps toward transformation. If you want results, do them. And don't move on to the next chapter until you have.

#1: Watch "Everybody Dies, But Not Everybody Lives" by Prince Ea:

Search for and watch this video on YouTube. Reflect on its message, then ask: *Am I truly living?* If you're not, what needs to change?

#2: Create a Mind Movie:

A mind movie is a short visual film of your desired future and dream self. You can create it on Canva, iMovie, or any editing app that you use on your phone or computer. Gather images and videos that highlight your ultimate reality. Who you are. How you show up. Your job. Your house. Your car. Be as specific as possible. Watch it every morning and every night. It will help you to cultivate a strong sense of self-belief and motivation to achieve your desires. In other words, it will help you start to take action. (You can find a direct link to learn more about this through the QR code at the end of this chapter.)

#3: Revisiting Activities:

Go back through this book. Complete any activities that you skipped. This is your real-world curriculum—take it seriously. No excuses. It holds the key to your personal and professional transformation. It has worked for all the co-authors of this book, the clients I have worked with over the years, and myself. (The bonus for you: This is the most perfected version. So, take advantage!)

#4: Find an Accountability Partner:

If you find yourself struggling to take action, then it's time to seek someone outside of yourself for encouragement. This could be a colleague, friend, family member, mentor, or counselor. Taking action becomes easier when we let somebody in who can offer us motivation, clarity, or inspiration.

#5: If You Are Still Struggling:

After finishing this book, if you are still struggling with taking action, you are probably blocked for a reason. In that case, you will want to read *The Gift* by Edith Eger. For now, just add it to your TBR (to be read) list.

A Call to Action for Leaders

Leadership will test your patience. Sometimes you'll encounter individuals who overanalyze, hesitate, or wait for explicit direction. The temptation to intervene and "just do it yourself" is strong, but you have to resist it. While you can guide, mentor, and coach—you cannot move people. They must choose to move themselves.

The old adage still holds true: "You can lead a horse to water, but you can't make it drink." And, in the world of business, if you force someone's head into the water, they'll either drown or resent you for it.

Instead, make sure you are doing the following:

#1: Empower Action and Initiative in Others:

Equip individuals to take their first microaction (Be a catalyst!), but don't carry them by doing it for them. Set clear expectations. Model decisiveness. Provide psychological safety. Give feedback. Be direct. And make sure to celebrate effort, not just ideal outcomes.

#2: Don't Be Done After Step One:

After encouraging someone to take action, your work isn't finished. They did *one* thing, but it hasn't become a habit yet, so they still need your support. Encourage them to take the next step or microaction, and if they don't know what that is, work with them to figure it out. Again, don't do it for them—you can catalyze the action, but they need to own it themselves.

#3: Implement SMART Goals:

Ensure that your objectives are Specific, Measurable, Achievable, Relevant, and Time-bound. Begin with a 90-day window. Then expand to one, three, and five-year horizons. Research indicates that clarity in goal-setting significantly enhances engagement, alignment, and results. When individuals know what they're aiming for and why, they begin to *act*—and they show up as leaders themselves.

#4: Don't Just Start and Forget:

If you are empowering someone by utilizing ideas one through three above, don't just start helping them and then totally forget about it. You fail as a leader if you do this. Why? Because they will plateau. So, set a reminder and follow up with them to see how they are doing with the microactions. Make them feel seen, heard, and supported.

#5: Make an Accountability Group:

Offer rising stars within your organization to be a part of an accountability group. This way, no one feels isolated—they're supported by others who are also working on taking growth-oriented actions. It doesn't have to take up an insane amount of time either. The group could meet one hour per month to update on goals and progress.

POWER WITHOUT PERMISSION

Scan this QR code to check out more resources.

Chapter 10: Developing Leadership Presence

"Leadership is about making others better as a result of your presence and making sure that impact lasts in your absence." — Sheryl Sandberg

At a certain stage in your career—particularly when aspiring toward the next echelon of the business world—the dialogue must evolve beyond yourself. It must also encompass others and how they perceive you. Your leadership presence—how you show up, speak, and carry yourself—is not a superficial add-on; it is the most vital expression of your capabilities. It gives you credibility, amplifies your influence, and ensures your memorability. In most cases, your leadership presence is the decisive factor when advancement opportunities arise or critical leadership roles need to be filled.

In this final chapter, we'll explore one of the most critical and frequently underestimated dimensions of professional growth: how you show up as a leader. This includes presence, but also extends beyond it to power, communication, and alignment. Whether you're consciously cultivating it or not, your professional presence is part of your personal brand. And, as you ascend in business, that brand precedes you in every room you walk into. You'll also hear from Marina, a peer whose executive presence is both felt and remembered. Her journey is a powerful example of the shift from capable to credible, from competence to influence.

Remember, presence isn't something you earn through permission or external validation—it's a choice. Each time you step fully into the room as yourself, you're claiming power without permission.

Building Confidence

Leadership starts with confidence—not the performative kind—the kind rooted in assurance of your identity and value. True confidence enables you to occupy space without apology, maintain eye contact, enter rooms with composure, and speak with clarity.

Confidence is like a muscle though. It needs training through consistent and intentional practice. Without this effort, it will remain underdeveloped.

You can start by making these two foundational shifts.

The Internal Shift: Redirect your focus from perceived deficiencies to your inherent strengths. Many of the high-performing women I coach habitually minimize their excellence. Conversely, many men I've come across almost always overstate theirs. If we could meet somewhere in the middle, we'd all be better for it.

The External Shift: Refine your physical presence. I've seen highly capable women diminish their impact by entering rooms hurried, disengaged, or visually withdrawn. Furthermore, how you dress, carry yourself, and greet people are not trivial—they're critical leadership tools. (First impressions set the hierarchical order!)

Here are several enduring truths I've gleaned about confidence over one and a half decades of executive development:

- Others take note of how you speak about yourself. If you lack belief in yourself, then how could others believe in you?
- So much of leadership presence is visual: body language, attire, facial expression, and spatial awareness.
- How you show up matters. Unsteady body language—like a weak handshake, poor posture, or scattered demeanor—signals doubt and uncertainty.
- People's presence, including how they dress, often shapes the way others perceive their leadership potential—and this goes for all genders! Dressing for where you're headed, rather than just where you are, is a subtle form of self-advocacy. It doesn't mean abandoning personal style or changing who you are; it just means being intentional. "Business casual" should never be mistaken

for athleisure or graphic tees, unless your industry norms allow it. For example, tech tends to be more relaxed. Rule of thumb: Aim for polished, not sloppy. (If you still want to hold on to your rebellious teenager view, fine. Just know, even if you sport a more youthful style, you still don't want to come across as sloppy. Although there may never be an outright discussion about it, how you dress does make an impact on people subconsciously.)
- Don't default to stereotypical gender behaviors. Show up with intention, not with the limiting expectations of how a woman "should" be or act. Remember that "authority" does not only equate to masculine energy.

Women are often conditioned to conflate visibility with arrogance, so they shy away from confidence, believing it may come across as cockiness. However, while cockiness is egoic, authentic confidence is *soulful*.

Mastering Communication and Negotiation

Communication and negotiation are essential tools for extending your influence and establishing authority. Many people struggle with them, or feel like they turn everything into a confrontation. I promise you though that both can be wielded effectively, and with sophistication.

Let's break down both concepts.

Effective Communication

Compelling verbal communication begins with preparation. You must know your stance and plan your key points. Then it's about how you deliver. Speak from your diaphragm instead of your throat (this way your voice carries strength instead of strain) and leverage the five Cs of communication. (There are many versions of the "Cs of communication," from three Cs to seven, but these are my personal favorites!)

- Clarity: Ensure your message is understandable.
- Conciseness: Stay on topic.

- Completeness: Support your message with context.
- Correctness: Ensure your message is accurate and factual.
- Courtesy: Be respectful of your audience.

Lastly, adapt these tips to whatever room you're in and the audience you find yourself with. For example, an all-male room may engage more directly or competitively with ideas, while a room full of women may prioritize connection and collaborative discussion. This doesn't mean one group is more capable than the other. It just means these are simply the norms we have inherited due to our culture and how each gender is socialized. Thus, tailoring your message will enhance your impact. Regardless of your audience, speak with confidence—and resist filling silence. (With the utmost politeness, this is your reminder to shut the f up when necessary!)

Remember: Communication isn't only verbal. Nonverbal communication is equally crucial. Your eyes, hands, posture (even how you tilt your head), all speak before your mouth does. So when you walk into a meeting, own the room with your presence before you even say a word. Take a prime seat that makes you feel uncomfortable to truly give yourself a seat at the table. (Talk about leadership confidence!)

Strategic Negotiation

Failing to negotiate means forfeiting money and power—whether it's for your salary or how to tackle a work project. A Pew Research survey found that 66% of job candidates got offered higher starting salaries simply by negotiating for more (Overvest, 2025). Unfortunately, many women hesitate, fearing negative perceptions or coming across as difficult.

Let me paint you two scenarios with Patty, a senior marketing manager:

Scenario 1: During a salary review meeting, she sat across from her department head, Kyle, and hesitantly began, "I was just hoping we could maybe talk about a raise… if that's okay." She avoided eye contact and nervously shifted in her seat. "I mean,

I've been working really hard on some campaigns, and I think they've done well... I'm not sure, but maybe I could be considered for something closer to $120,000?" Her voice trailed off, and she quickly added, "But if that's too much, I totally understand—whatever works for the budget."

Scenario 2: During her salary review meeting, Patty confidently stated, "Over the past year, I've led two high-impact campaigns that increased client engagement by roughly 40%, directly contributing to a 15% revenue increase." While speaking, she maintained eye contact and sat with an open posture. "Based on market benchmarks for my role and performance outcomes, a salary of $120,000 reflects the value I bring to the company. I'd also like to discuss opportunities for equity participation, as I'm committed to growing with the organization long-term."

I'm not even going to ask you who is more likely to get the raise. Patty from Scenario 1 didn't cite accomplishments or share market data. Her uncertainty made it easy to dismiss her request. Patty from Scenario 2, however, was calm and assertive. Did you notice that she had no filler words? Or how she was professional and self-assured? Furthermore, she wasn't demanding, but left space for a collaborative conversation with Kyle.

While Patty and Kyle are fictional, I've witnessed these scenarios countless times. I have had these *exact* interactions countless times—and I was always much more convinced by women who presented themselves like Patty in the second scenario.

The truth is, no one's coming to save you—it's time to negotiate on your own behalf. As you can see, negotiation does not mean *combat*—it is simply *a type of communication* that requires clarity, confidence, and preparation. Know your worth. Back your requests with data. Pose thoughtful, clarifying questions. And ask—assertively and unapologetically.

Authentic Leadership

When developing your leadership presence, don't look to others or mimic outdated models of authority. In fact, you should do the opposite and embody your own unique expression. Studies show that up to 70% of employee engagement is directly influenced by leadership behavior (Royal, 2019). This isn't just about you feeling your best—it's about the ripple effect your leadership has on others. Your team will be far more inspired by your authenticity than your fakeness in trying to be someone you're not. I've said this before and I'll say it again: Fakeness and manipulation are seen and felt—if not immediately, then eventually, and by everyone. Please don't be that person. To lead authentically, start by redefining what "authority" looks like for you. You don't have to yell, dominate, or act like the loudest person in the room. Some of the most respected leaders I know speak with quiet certainty—and are heard by all. Instead, be warm and firm.

Leadership, at its best, integrates qualities that are traditionally labeled as masculine or feminine—but are ultimately human and not mutually exclusive. You can be nurturing and commanding. You can be direct and compassionate. You can take up space and remain grounded. These qualities don't need to *compete*—they *complement* each other. To lead from a place of wholeness requires both.

Marina's Story: The Chair She Built Herself

When Marina walks into a room, you notice her—not because she demands attention, but because her confident posture and grounded energy naturally command it. These skills weren't innate; she built them through intentional and consistent development.

> *As an executive and senior leader today, I can tell you my path to leadership presence wasn't paved through boardrooms and corner offices. It was paved through years of life experiences that tested*

everything I thought I knew about myself—from learning resilience and grit as emotional survival tools to battling the instinct to hide rather than take space in rooms where I felt I didn't belong.

I spent my early childhood in Stockton, California. It was recognized for decades as one of the worst cities in the nation and was ranked by Forbes as America's fifth most dangerous city. For years, I avoided telling people where I was from, knowing it often drew immediate disdain and distrust.

Many of my early childhood and teen experiences in Stockton left me hardened. It's where I survived my most painful experiences and learned that vulnerability was a liability, toughness a necessity. Plus, as the firstborn child, I carried an innate sense of responsibility to protect. I knew firsthand that the world—and often people in authority—offered no safety.

My guard stayed up—especially since we never stayed at any house too long, and I attended fifteen schools before graduating high school. I developed a system: smile, appear confident, and observe those around me. Over time, I learned to be surface-friendly with everyone, but kept people at a distance. This constant adaptation taught me to read rooms instantly and become whatever was needed to survive.

Everything shifted my junior year though, when my father—who for most of my life was continuing his medical education, doing residencies and internships that kept us living modestly—established his private practice. We moved to affluent Claremont, California, into our dream custom home. It was a far cry from some of the apartments we had lived in previously.

That drastic shift in socioeconomic status as a teen gave me perspective. I had lived at two ends of the spectrum: from lower income to affluent, from friends who were gang members to friends who drove Porsches. It was my first leadership lesson: I became comfortable around anyone—any race, income level, or situation.

Ironically, though, the world didn't always seem as accepting of me. Having been raised in different ethnic cultures, I struggled to navigate my own identity. I often felt like I existed in the margins— not fully this, not fully that. And my family had to overcome cruel stereotypes and horrible treatment from strangers. It created a quiet, internal dissonance that fueled both my anger at power abuse and my drive to overachieve.

Despite the cruel treatment, violence, and financial hardship in my early life, I remained ambitious. While attending USC as a full-time student, I worked three jobs: commercial real estate by day, legal transcription at night, and emergency room shifts on weekends. I thrived under constant pressure and fell in love with working and being excellent at everything I touched.

After graduating, I remained in the commercial real estate industry for eight years. It was dynamic and challenging, and everything about it intrigued me. The idea of something concrete being formed from dirt gave me hope for my own life.

And that hope took root in my early twenties, when a major pivot took place. First, I converted to Christianity. Second, with encouragement from my college best friend, I began therapy. Therapy was taboo in my culture, so my parents didn't understand or support it, but I knew I was doing the right thing.

If I wanted to level up, I had to put to bed the pain that had haunted me for years.

Through both shifts, I discovered the power of love and forgiveness. I stopped blaming myself for things beyond my control and found grace for poor choices made from pain. Getting to the truth of my trauma was freeing—I could finally chase joy and design my own life.

A few years later, I met my husband and became a stay-at-home mom for ten years. That season taught me a new kind of leadership: managing human beings through constantly changing stages of development. It required me to be a nurturer, disciplinarian, teacher, coach, manager, and motivator—and I learned something powerful from my husband. His leadership at home and as a father was quiet but commanding—a form of soft power I hadn't witnessed before. I realized true strength didn't have to be loud, intimidating, or forceful. And over time, I integrated that approach into my own leadership style.

That lesson proved invaluable when I later led mission teams. During one particularly challenging experience, I found myself navigating between competing interests—my team's goals, my church's reputation, and the host organization's mission. I worked one-on-one with the frustrated founder, remaining calm and unoffended during difficult conversations, while helping my hurt team see how to add value in new ways and gain the most from a difficult situation. I helped create a plan that served both sides and taught critical leadership lessons for future success. That founder later became one of my closest friends and told me, "I have met hundreds of pastors and leaders over these decades, and I have never met anyone who led with your strength and grace without ever losing your cool, even when I gave some pretty harsh feedback." I even went on to mentor her from a leadership perspective.

When I finally re-entered the workforce, I transitioned into manufacturing, joining a $25 million privately held company. Over twelve years, I worked through five major acquisitions and mergers, growing the enterprise to $500 million before it was sold. It was high-stakes, high-stress work with long hours and moving targets. I learned a lot about leadership in the process: to deal with unexpected problems quickly and directly, to be willing to adapt, and to always move the team forward.

One of the most defining moments came during a $75 million merger between two competing manufacturers. In the midst of executing our transition plan, we missed a critical customer forecast for their nationwide promotion. While sales and production were at war, each blaming the other for an impossible situation—requiring three overtime shifts on a holiday weekend—I focused on not failing this customer and secured approval for the additional costs.

Though it wasn't my fault, I walked into a meeting and said, "This is my fault" knowing the production team would move mountains to save me— something they wouldn't do for the person truly at fault. The response was immediate: They appreciated that I would take the hit for the cost overruns, knowing that only they could save the company from "my error."

My practice of giving company-wide recognition to every team's contributions had built relationships that could withstand crises. They were willing to work those brutal holiday shifts because, as one supervisor told me later, they knew I had always *had their back. That moment taught me leadership isn't about being right—it's about building trust that drives extraordinary results.*

Despite my success, I kept battling the narrative that I was "damaged goods." With so few women of color in corporate leadership, not seeing myself reflected only reinforced my insecurities about belonging. It was harder still to watch others who brought little value show no doubts about belonging. There were numerous men at the highest levels who were extremely underqualified, yet arrived by connection and had unwavering confidence. That awareness led me to invest in a leadership coach, Andreas.

In just a few short months of working with him, I underwent a major transformation. He believed in me before I could fully believe in myself, showing me I wasn't becoming someone new—I was unveiling who I'd always been, chiseling away every voice that told me to be smaller. I learned that in any room, power comes not from a title, but from communicating with poise and precision.

That realization guided me soon after, when we faced a massive workplace disruption. False accusations about an inappropriate relationship between two employees—one a key leader—required investigating thirteen people and uncovering the real issue: Our first female star performer in a traditionally male company was struggling with insecurity when another strong woman joined the team.

Years earlier, I'd have recommended termination, but my evolved approach sought win-win solutions. People are human first, and effective leadership requires empathy. I recognized her behavior stemmed from personal struggles affecting her work perspective. Through patient one-on-one coaching, I helped her separate facts from the meanings she'd assigned, rebuilding her understanding of interactions she'd misinterpreted due to personal insecurities. My team later acknowledged that I reached someone no one else could connect with, resolving what seemed impossible.

After that, I felt I could conquer anything. Doors opened in unprecedented ways. I walked with a new confidence that elevated everything—my leadership presence, my personal relationships, and my roles as wife and mother.

Today, I serve as Senior VP of Operations at a leading manufacturer's rep agency, managing multiple companies and averaging at least two M&A transactions a year. My journey has been one of unlayering—shedding survival mechanisms, dismantling trauma, rewriting narratives, and stepping into my value. And the confidence I have today isn't false confidence borrowed from a title. It's from knowing that I am a diamond. A diamond doesn't need light to be brilliant—only to be uncovered. And the one covering this diamond was me. I didn't become worthy—I was always worthy. I had just been hiding myself for too long. That's where true leadership presence gets forged: When your voice, your values, and your unshakeable knowing that you belong all come into alignment.

So, if I could offer advice to any woman entering the executive arena, it would be this:

First, check your language. Many women say that they are "waiting" for a seat at the table. Those words were once part of my vocabulary, too. But not anymore. When I pull up my own chair, it's a chair I built. I own it. I forged it. I occupy it. It's imperative to have confidence in what you bring to the table and take pride in the fact that your voice doesn't sound like everyone else's.

Second, invest in a coach. That was truly one of the greatest investments I have ever made. Andreas challenged me regularly, pushed me beyond my levels of comfort, and helped me unveil who I've always been on the inside. I'm grateful to call him a friend today.

Third, recognize your value. You possess experience and perspective that others don't. You can lift people with your words, your eyes, and your intuition. Recognize the diamond within yourself. Your leadership presence isn't something to develop externally—it's something to uncover internally.

As Marina's journey illustrates, leadership presence is cultivated (not inherited!) through confidence, self-awareness, and deliberate practice. Consider how you're showing up. Not just at work, but in every aspect of your life.

Activities for Developing Leadership Presence

Leadership presence is not about being the most vocal, polished, or perfect. It's about alignment between who you are and how you lead. It's about translating invisible qualities (like confidence, conviction, and clarity) into real-world impact. It's about building a commanding personal brand that speaks louder than a resume ever could.

Here are some exercises to strengthen this presence. Don't move on to the next chapter until you've done them.

#1: Always Show Up as a Leader:

No matter what room you enter, you can make it a point to show up as a leader—even if right now you're only leading yourself. You never know who might be in the room! Carry yourself with authenticity and confidence, and you'll already have a leg up.

#2: Redefine Authority:

Earlier I mentioned the importance of redefining authority. Spend 15 minutes journaling about this. Write down your personal mission, vision, and values, according to your new definition of authority. Anchor into them—that's what makes your presence uniquely powerful.

#3: Practice Active Listening:

Not only in your next conversation but for the next week, focus on *active* listening. Silence distractions. Maintain eye contact. Ask thoughtful questions. Truly listen instead of planning out your response. This builds trust and enhances your presence.

#4: Practice Negotiating:

If negotiating is not a skill you have honed yet, then it's time to start practicing to be like the Patty from scenario two. You can do this with a friend or in the mirror. Practice one of these negotiation conversations: (1) Ask your manager for a raise. (2) Negotiate your starting salary at a new company.

#5: Seek Feedback:

We all have blind spots. We might think we're presenting ourselves one way, but are actually presenting ourselves in an entirely different way. Ask trusted colleagues how you're perceived in the office. Once you've gained insights and gathered data, note areas you'd like to work on—whether it's your energy, your attire, or your body language.

Call to Action for Leaders

Leadership presence isn't merely a personal journey that some people embark on—it's imperative for the collective. Organizations thrive when leadership pipelines are diverse and inclusive, and employees are more likely to step up if they are given the support and opportunities to do so.

#1: An Activity Specifically For Men:

If you're a man in a position of influence, start creating opportunities for women. Even small actions create big impacts. Let her walk into the room first. Encourage peers to shake her hand before yours. Elevate her voice in meetings. You can make this look effortless: simply walk into a room at a slower pace, physically lower your hand, and highlight her great points.

When I shared this concept with a female colleague, she asked, "How many men *actually* do that?" Her response was sobering. These behaviors should not be *rare*—they should be *standard*. Men: Don't take up space if you don't need to.

#2: Create Mentorship Programs:

No one learns to lead alone. Leadership presence is developed and nurtured in community. So pair emerging talent with mentors who can provide feedback, encouragement, and perspective. Growth happens in environments that invest in potential.

#3: Be Mindful and Don't Correct Women:

Women have lived their entire lives being corrected by, sneered at, or looked down upon by condescending men. Be mindful—and don't add to this narrative. Only correct a woman if it's business critical. Other than that, stop. And, if you find that you *do* have to correct a woman's course of action, do not do it in front of anyone else. Pull her aside and speak to her privately. Be warm and firm in your approach.

#4: Bring an Up-and-Coming Woman In:

If you have a standout female talent at the company, bring her into a higher-level meeting. Even if it's just to listen rather than participate, it'll give her something to aspire to and start her leadership track.

#5: Give Equal Praise:

Do not only praise men. Praise women and men equally and honestly. This strengthens *everyone's* positions in the room. Plus, it helps women see that their efforts are being noticed and that they're equal to the men around them.

Scan this QR code to check out more resources.

Section IV: Purpose & Transformation
Emerge as a Polished Diamond

Chapter 11: Leading with Purpose and Vision

> *"Leadership is the capacity to influence others through inspiration, motivated by passion, generated by vision, produced by a conviction, ignited by a purpose."* — Myles Munroe

At this point in the book—and your journey—a pivotal shift occurs. You've done the internal work in Section II: Awareness (which relates to the Aspiring Zone) and executed strategic moves in Section III: Direction and Action (which relates to the Growing Zone). Now you reach what senior leaders call an inflection point—when growth transcends personal advancement and starts creating systemic impact.

Welcome to Section IV: Purpose and Transformation (which will help you reach the Thriving Zone). This is the moment your evolution extends beyond you—to the teams you lead, the organizations you shape, and the future you will help build.

You didn't come this far just to run high-performance meetings or climb another rung on the corporate ladder. You're here to align your work with your values, lead with intention, and show up each day rooted in your *why*—why you lead, why your team exists, why your goals matter, and why your contributions are significant. When leadership is fueled by clarity, conviction, and core values, people don't just comply—they become inspired and ignited themselves.

In this chapter, we're going to discuss purpose (your internal compass) and vision (your external North Star), and examine how these forces converge to produce transformational leadership. You'll also hear from my colleague Alyssa—a visionary with strategic foresight and the ability to galvanize others.

Defining and Discovering Purpose

"Find your purpose" is a phrase that's repeated often yet rarely deconstructed. What does *purpose* truly mean? And how does one find it? (Don't worry—if you're not sure yet, the activities at the end of this chapter will help you.)

Purpose, in its most authentic form, emerges through a process of introspection and lived experience. It often begins with reflection—on core values, personal interests, defining experiences, and moments of adversity—and unfolds as you explore new challenges, opportunities, and communities. It is less a sudden epiphany and more a gradual unveiling of what was already embedded in your life story all along.

Often, our purpose is born from resilience in what we've overcome. In the aftermath of said hardship, we gain insights that allow us to guide others through similar terrain. That is the essence of service-driven leadership.

For example, as you read in Chapter 1, my purpose is to help those who are like my mother: amazing people who are struggling—whether that be financially, professionally, or personally. It was so difficult as a young child to witness the most beautiful and intelligent person I knew barely keeping a roof over our head and rarely getting opportunities in life. That life path was mine so that I *could* overcome that pain and figure out how to position myself to make a difference—one person at a time. And that's why I love what I do every day. I am doing the service that was meant for me, that lights me up from the inside.

Not everyone feels a clear or singular sense of purpose—and that's entirely valid. In such cases, anchoring yourself to your core values is an effective starting point. Ask yourself: Why am I choosing to spend my time this way? Does this align with who I want to become? Is this worth my life energy? Does this feel right?

Regardless of whether your purpose feels fully defined or still emerging, let your "why" inform your daily decisions and actions. Since we devote more time to work than any other activity, the imperative is clear: Make your work worth it and enjoy the process.

Crafting a Vision for the Future

Purpose, while vital, must be coupled with vision. That's the only way to convert internal ideas to external outcomes. Why? Because vision provides direction.

Some individuals—visionaries—possess a natural aptitude for foresight, seeing the future as a vivid landscape of possibility. But vision alone is merely imagination—and that's where they can falter. You don't need to be a grand strategist, but you do need to develop short-, mid-, and long-term goals that reflect your broader purpose. True leadership is the ability to articulate your vision clearly and compellingly so others are eager to follow—because you're not just achieving results, you're building meaning.

Establishing your vision doesn't mean you'll have it all figured out. Course correction will be needed from time to time. If a goal loses resonance, pivot. The right path is typically the one that gives life, not drains it.

Balancing Dualities: Personal and Inclusive Leadership

Thriving leadership demands the rare ability to hold dualities: to be both grounded and aspirational, directive and empathetic, firm in principle yet warm in approach. For example, true leaders possess *strong* opinions, yet hold them *loosely* to remain open and approachable. I've observed that, in general, men are socialized to hold strong opinions strongly. While women are often conditioned to hold loose opinions loosely. We must evolve out of these ingrained patterns. We must allow for both masculine and feminine energies to coexist. That's where real leadership lives.

This duality also exists at the intersection of personal leadership and inclusive leadership—because it isn't only about you or others, but always about both at the same time. Personal leadership centers around self-governance—your emotional intelligence, self-awareness, and growth mindset. Your level of personal development is the blueprint that your team will often emulate. Inclusive leadership, on the other hand, is about fostering empathy, collaboration, and belonging to create a culture where diverse perspectives thrive and each voice holds value.

Think of it like this: When it comes to personal leadership, you're the captain of the ship. When it comes to inclusive leadership, you're the DJ on its booze cruise—steering the course while curating the experience for everyone aboard. When you lead in this integrated fashion, the people around you will sense it and rise to meet it. Why? Because it is *real*, and real is *rare*.

This isn't just theory—the data on this subject backs it up. Harvard Business Review found that companies with strong, balanced leaders drive 73% higher innovation revenue and 36% higher profitability (Zheng, et al., 2023). Therefore, someone skilled in both personal and inclusive leadership—who emphasizes self-awareness and a diverse culture—will no doubt achieve better results in their lives, in their businesses, or across their organization.

Alyssa's Story: The Transformation Imperative

Alyssa resists stagnation and dismantles systems that don't serve people well. She imagines bold futures—in any industry, business, or room—and guides others toward them with clarity and courage. That's why I want you to hear her story.

> *The conference line fell silent. I'd just lost my composure in front of the executive team, fighting to save key members of my marketing team from a 40% workforce reduction. These weren't just employees—they were people who'd given everything to build our company.*
>
> *As the words to save those few key employees tumbled out—passionate, though maybe too forceful—I could feel my credibility slipping away.*

The very qualities that had made me successful—my fierce loyalty, my refusal to accept "that's just business"—were now working against me. Five months later, I was laid off.

Do I regret standing up for my team? Never. Do I wish I'd calibrated my approach better? Absolutely.

That boardroom moment became a turning point in how I understood leadership. Through years of navigating acquisitions and corporate change, I'd always led with passion and conviction. But this experience taught me the importance of staying true to your values while adapting how you express them. It was a lesson I'd carry forward into every role that followed.

My ability to see that painful exit not as failure but as a learning moment traces back to five words my mother said every morning before school: "Make it a great day."

Not "have" a great day—make it.

That subtle shift in language—from passive recipient to active creator—became my North Star through decades of corporate transformation. But the truth is, this mindset wasn't just philosophical for me. It was survival.

Growing up in a blue-collar family living paycheck to paycheck, I learned early that circumstances don't define you—your response to them does. My mother's daily reminder taught me to stay grounded in reality while maintaining an optimistic outlook. I knew there would be no handouts or safety nets waiting for me. Everything I wanted, I'd have to fight for. But rather than let circumstances or predefined paths limit my future, I chose to create my own.

This reality lit a fire inside me. When I discovered something I was passionate about, I became relentless—want it, work for it, own it.

This fierce drive showed up early. In sixth grade, when I auditioned for Scrooge in our school play, it never occurred to me that a girl playing a male lead might be unusual. I wanted that role with an intensity that surprised even me. I rehearsed until my family begged for mercy—And I got the part.

Later that year, when I didn't land the lead role in the spring musical "Alice in Wonderland," I could have felt sorry for myself. But instead, I transformed my part of the Caterpillar into such a scene-stealer that my performance earned me a standing ovation and an overwhelming amount of fan mail from the kindergarten class.

Looking back, I realize I was already learning something important. That sixth-grade caterpillar wasn't a consolation prize—it was proof that when you can't get the role you want, you transform the role you have. I didn't just play the part—I made it unforgettable.

"Want it. Work for it. Own it." This mantra would define my entire career.

After a decade working in PR agencies, I found my true calling as a marketer in the startup world. My first CEO in that space had a philosophy that rewired my understanding of leadership: "I want to make this a career-defining moment for as many people as possible," he would say.

Not just for himself. Not just for investors. For as many people as possible.

For six years, I poured everything into that vision. The late nights and impossible deadlines were worth it because we were building something together. That euphoric feeling of a team in perfect sync, crushing goals together—it's intoxicating.

After a roller coaster ride, filled with the highest of highs and a few lows, my first startup was finally acquired in 2017, validating everything we'd built together. But as an early employee deeply invested in our mission, I'd lost myself in the dream of it all.

When the moment finally arrived, reality hit differently than I'd imagined. Yes, there was the euphoria of success, the vindication of relentless work, the financial reward. But there was also something I hadn't anticipated: grief. Our amazing culture would be absorbed into a larger machine. People might lose their jobs. The magic we'd created together would never be quite the same.

Two women on my team became my anchors during that whirlwind. One had already survived five acquisitions. Shortly after our announcement, she shared some hard-won wisdom: "You have a choice here. Think about what you want from this. Do you see yourself at this new company? Are you passionate about what they do?"

Her words reframed the experience and crystallized what I'd been feeling: An acquisition wasn't something happening to us—it was something we could navigate on our own terms. While this was an incredible journey, I realized this was where my chapter ended.

That first acquisition taught me something crucial: Success can be bittersweet, and that's okay. The end of one journey is just the beginning of another. The key is recognizing when it's time to turn the page.

I proactively landed a role as head of marketing at another startup, led by a former COO.

It was a soft landing with familiar faces and a natural next step. Little did I know it would be the beginning of a pattern—four more successful exits over the next seven years.

Throughout all the reorgs, acquisitions, and layoffs, one truth became undeniable: Relationships are your real career capital. Titles disappear, companies get acquired, strategies pivot—but the people who've seen you at your best and worst, who've fought alongside you in the trenches, endure.

I've had a COO who became my next CEO. Team members who became career-long mentors. Peers and direct reports who were my first calls when I was building a new team at a new company. Each relationship was an investment that paid dividends across multiple companies.

Remember those two women who were my anchors during my first acquisition? Three years later, we joined a new company with our former CEO, who actively recruited us. Together, we navigated COVID, survived another acquisition, and made a pact to truly support each other. Weekly meetings became our lifeline—sharing fears, celebrating wins, strategizing next moves. While others scrambled up constantly restructuring ladders, we built something more valuable: an unshakeable support network that would outlast any single company.

Each acquisition taught me to refine my approach without losing my essence. The clearest example came during my time with CEO Andreas Pettersson. I'd identified a critical need and wanted our company to revisit our Ideal Customer Profile (ICP). But instead of charging into our annual planning session with guns blazing (like my early-career boardroom blow up approach), Andreas helped me strategize. We discussed how to socialize the idea and present it in a way that invited collaboration rather than resistance.

The project was approved, and it transformed our go-to-market strategy. More importantly, it showed me what calibrated leadership looks like: same passion, same conviction, but delivered in a way that brings people along rather than putting them on defense.

Andreas didn't just tolerate my fearlessness and relationship-driven approach—he celebrated it. Under his leadership, I reached my full potential precisely because I could lead authentically while adapting my style to the situation.

But here's what I've learned: As we climb the corporate ladder, we're often asked to leave that fearlessness behind—to play it safe, to conform. The most successful leaders I know have learned to calibrate without compromising their authentic strengths.

And the corporate world, which is transforming at breakneck speed—AI disruption, global teams, hybrid work environments, constant M&A activity—demands leaders who can adapt without losing themselves, who bring empathy alongside strategy, who build genuine relationships while driving hard results.

These leaders—the ones who naturally balance analytical thinking with emotional intelligence, who see vulnerability as strength, not weakness—they're often women. Not always, but often enough that it matters.

And too many of us still feel pressure to suppress these qualities to fit traditional corporate molds. That's exactly backward.

Here's your playbook for leading through change without losing yourself:

Reclaim your fearlessness. *Channel that inner child who didn't know what he or she couldn't do.*

Master calibration, not conformity. *Learn to read the room without silencing your voice.*

Invest in relationships before you need them. *Your network isn't just who you know—it's who will advocate for you when everything changes.*

Know when to turn the page. *There's a difference between running from discomfort versus leaving because you've learned all you can.*

Find environments that value your strengths. *If you're constantly asked to be someone you're not, you're in the wrong place.*

Remember: You make your day. *When change feels overwhelming, when the ground shifts beneath you yet again, remember that you can let circumstances define you, or you can make it a great day anyway.*

After five acquisitions and navigating countless changes, I finally understood what my mother meant about "making" your day. Every leader faces this choice: Remain comfortable in familiar patterns, or embrace the messy, beautiful process of growth and change.

Remember the sixth-grader who transformed that small Caterpillar role into something unforgettable? That was my first proof of my mother's "make it a great day" theory. And her theory proved its worth. When you can't change your circumstances, you change your mindset. When you can't get the role you want, you transform the role you have. When the world demands conformity, you choose evolution instead.

> *In a world of constant change, the ability to adapt while staying true to yourself isn't just a nice leadership quality. It's your superpower. And the corporate world has never needed it more.*

While many dwell on the past—regretting, replaying, rehashing—Alyssa looks forward, reminding us that our best work still lies ahead of us. You'll know you're operating in this way when you feel aligned and energized by your work. If you truly care about something, you are going to put your all into it. If you don't, then it probably isn't part of your purpose.

Activities for Leading with Purpose and Vision

Purpose and vision are all about authenticity and direction. Here are some essential exercises that can help you master this. Don't move on to the next chapter until you've done them.

#1: Create a Vision Statement:

Write a clear statement articulating the who, what, where, when, and why of your future goals. This will serve as your personal and professional North Star. Share it with those around you. You'll know you have it when you are excited about it and do anything you can in your free time to move it forward.

#2: Make a Vision Board:

Similar to the vision statement, but this time with pictures, design a visual representation of your aspirations. This will serve as your daily reminder of where you are headed.

#3: Find Your North Star:

Read my ebook *Find Your North Star: 12 Steps to Unlock Clarity, Purpose, and Success*. This ebook is free and available on my website. It's all about finding your vision and purpose.

#4: Write a Letter from the Future:

Just as we can gather lots of insight by looking into the past, we can gain insight by looking into the future. Write a letter from your future self to your present self, describing the accomplishments you've achieved and the ways you've grown over the past few years. Let it inspire you to walk toward that vision.

#5: Journal about Your Role Model:

A great way to enhance our lives and leadership is by analyzing why we admire certain people. Who is your role model? What qualities do they have that you aspire to cultivate in yourself? How could you tap more into their leadership abilities with your own authentic approach?

As you do these exercises, remember that success can be multidimensional. It's not always about more money. I've seen professionals leave renowned global firms—accepting 30% pay cuts—to return to purpose-driven cultures. Why? Because those environments demanded conformity and inauthenticity, forcing them to be cold and performative. They eventually realized that prestige without authenticity was unfulfilling and not worth pursuing.

Call to Action for Leaders

Great leaders evolve and catalyze evolution in others. Reflect not only on your own purpose and vision, but also on how you help others fine-tune theirs. So make sure you are doing the following.

#1: Reflect on Your Vision and Purpose:

Are you growing? Are those around you growing? Is your organization cultivating trust, safety, and authenticity? Are you leading with purpose and vision… or is it time to realign yourself?

#2: Read *The Five Dysfunctions of a Team* by Patrick Lencioni:

Evaluate your team based on the dysfunctions he outlines: absence of trust, fear of conflict, lack of commitment, avoidance of accountability, and inattention to results. Which dysfunctions are present? What conversations need to happen? Address root causes by building psychological safety, modeling accountability, and fostering a culture of open dialogue and celebration.

#3: Engage in Strategic Foresight:

Discuss industry trends, emerging challenges, and shared aspirations. Ask: What do we want to build? What are we excited about? What are we avoiding out of fear? Which women can we empower to lead this initiative? This kind of dialogue generates ambition and innovation, along with visionary thinking.

#4: Goal Mapping Group Activity:

Gather small teams to map out goals, focusing on both vision and purpose. Check in on each group to ensure *everyone* is participating equally. This will give quieter, less confident individuals a chance to build confidence and leadership skills. (When you choose team leads, make sure to choose women too!)

#5: Create a Company Vision Board:

Just as I recommend that people create vision boards for their own personal lives and goals, I recommend that companies create vision boards for future business goals. Find an empty or lonely wall somewhere in the office. Put up a bulletin board and encourage everyone to print pictures or quotes to tack onto the board. As an organization, you will create a collage of the future you want to strive for, together.

ANDREAS PETTERSSON

Scan this QR code to check out more resources.

Chapter 12: Overcoming Gender Discrepancies in the Workplace

"Life doesn't always give us what we deserve, but rather, what we demand. And so you must continue to push harder than any other person in the room." — Wadi Ben-Hirki

Despite decades of social advancement and professional reform, gender discrepancies remain a pervasive reality in today's professional landscape. They show up as unequal pay, underrepresentation in leadership, and subtler harms like microaggressions, exclusion from informal networks, and unconscious bias.

In other words, the playing field is far from level. While the illusion of equality may be convenient for some to believe, data and lived experience say otherwise. According to the U.S. Census Bureau, women in 2023 earned just 83 cents for every dollar their male counterparts made—and this statistic is even more alarming because women outnumber men in having a college education (AAUW, 2024).

For generations, women have been taught to wait for approval before speaking, leading, or making bold moves. But leadership grows when you stop waiting—when you claim your power without permission.

This chapter will shed light on these systemic challenges that continue to hold women back and provide actionable strategies for overcoming them. We will address everything from the boys' club culture and the glass ceiling to the essential role of male allies and the confidence gap. You'll also hear from Janne, whose career journey transformed from exclusion from a boys' club culture to leading inclusive, thriving teams where men and women grow side-by-side.

The Boys' Club Culture

The boys' club is not a myth—it's a living, breathing culture that exists in far too many organizations today. (I've personally seen it in action time and time again.) It's an informal network built on after-hours drinks and golf course handshakes—where business decisions get made outside the office. And it holds the unspoken assumption that leadership should look and sound a certain way—and that way is usually male.

Navigating the boys' club is both demanding and challenging for women and minorities. While waiting for change, they endure toxic environments that question them and make them feel invisible—requiring immense resilience. They have to endure subtle exclusionary behaviors—like seating arrangements or the order of who gets addressed in meetings—which naturally discourage ambition, but also overt attempts at power exertion, where men may use their body, voice, or status to intimidate. (Think: Angry dad.)

What's often overlooked, too, is the broader impact of these exclusionary dynamics. Yes, they disproportionately harm women and minorities—but that isn't the only harm they cause. They hinder innovation, limit diversity of thought, suppress morale, damage long-term performance, and perpetuate the glass ceiling. Organizations that solely run on male leadership are less adaptable, less empathetic, and less effective at solving complex problems.

This topic has a special place in my heart because my biggest failure in the business world was never getting a woman into the C-suite when I was CEO of a tech company, looking to expand the leadership team. It wasn't for a lack of trying though. I actually put a lot of effort into finding the right female leader for the job. However, some of the qualified candidates I liked were rejected by people above me. One woman, who they did approve of, didn't take the job because they refused to pay her the salary she asked for (which was less than what we paid for the male leader we ended up hiring, by the way). Others I interviewed simply lacked the necessary qualifications, and I couldn't hire them solely based on their gender—especially given the rejection of even the most qualified women. This personal failure has fueled in me the desire to relentlessly educate men and help women elevate themselves (hence, writing this book). I want there to be more awareness of gender biases and I want there to be more C-suite options. Only then will more companies fill these roles with qualified women.

So, let's break the glass ceiling and shed light on the barriers women face.

Breaking the Glass Ceiling

Despite their performance, qualifications, and achievements, many women find their careers capped in unspoken and unwritten ways. The "glass ceiling," a term coined in the '70s that still applies today, refers to these barriers—unconscious bias, unequal pay, and so on—that prevent women from reaching top leadership roles. Shockingly, for every 100 men who get promoted, only 72 women get promoted, meaning women are much more likely to remain in entry-level positions (Lean In, 2019). Another staggering statistic: Women held only 26% of C-suite positions in 2022, and just 5% of those were held by women of color (Dorsey, 2023).

There are a few clear ways leaders can dismantle these invisible barriers.

#1: Sponsorship over mentorship: Women need mentors, yes. But more than that, they need sponsors—leaders who will advocate for them behind closed doors and help them gain visibility where it matters to create new roles and opportunities for women.

#2: Addressing Unconscious Bias: We must move beyond overt discrimination and surface the hidden biases that shape hiring, promotions, and decision-making. Organizations can address this by diversifying hiring panels and offering gender bias training.

#3: Promoting Women: Empowering women in leadership benefits everyone—driving innovation, empathy, profitability, and inspiring other women to thrive.

The Role of Allyship

Systemic change to dismantle the boys' club, the glass ceiling, and unconscious biases cannot happen without men—hence the importance of male allyship.

Male allies use their influence to create opportunities for others. They don't just mentor—they sponsor. They advocate for women in rooms where they are absent. They ensure women's ideas get equal weight in meetings. They interrupt microaggressions and redirect conversations when women are talked over or minimized. They make sure promotions, raises, and projects aren't confined to the "inner circle." They champion policies that support gender equity—equal pay, flexible work arrangements, and robust anti-harassment measures.

Most importantly, male allies practice awareness. Many men, often unknowingly, hold more authority simply because of how others respond to their voices. (Angry dad!) Recognizing this dynamic is the first step toward dismantling it—along with holding themselves and their peers accountable.

But allyship is not just the job of men. As I've discussed early in the book, and as you've heard from some of the women's stories, women must become each other's allies too. That means no more scarcity, competition, or comparison. Female allyship means amplifying each other's ideas, sharing opportunities, and mentoring or sponsoring one another. You don't have to be best friends with every woman you work with—but you do have a responsibility not to undermine, diminish, or ignore the very people fighting the same fight you are.

The Confidence and Advocacy Gap

The confidence and advocacy gap is one of the most persistent internal challenges women face at work. It refers to the hesitation many women experience when it comes to owning their success, advocating for themselves, or applying for leadership roles.

But let's be clear: Part of this goes beyond women's control. Many job descriptions are written with an unconscious bias toward males. Leaders must ask themselves when hiring: What does this role truly require? What language might unintentionally exclude qualified women? Addressing these questions expands access to opportunities and creates a more equitable playing field.

And what part of this *is* in women's control? Giving themselves more permission. No matter how talented, skilled, or educated you are... if you can't back yourself, negotiate for yourself, or speak with authority, you will always be at a disadvantage. Maybe you've heard this statistic that received a lot of buzz some years back: Men are likely to apply for a role even if they meet just 60% of the qualifications, while women wait until they meet 100% of them. While this statistic by Mohr (2014) was more speculative than quantitative, Mohr found that women across different age groups had a higher fear of failing than men (22% vs. 13%), likely influencing when and how they consider applying for positions (Salwender, M. & Stahlberg, D., 2024).

So if you want to thrive in leadership, stop undervaluing your worth. Apply anyway. Apply even when you don't meet 100% of the qualifications. Trust your voice. Take up space. Know that your ideas matter. Stay grounded in your values. And never hand your power away to someone else. That is how you can become a respected leader.

Janne's Story: Extending a Hand, Building Equal Rooms

Few stories capture true resilience more powerfully than Janne's. A courageous, heart-centered leader, she has spent decades leading with strength, vision, and respect for all. We worked together in an environment still entrenched in traditional, male-dominated norms, yet she refused to choose between "being strong" or "being feminine," instead exemplifying both fiercely. Her story is one of courage that has paved the way for more equality between men and women.

ANDREAS PETTERSSON

I came of age in Denmark during the 1970s and '80s. My parents separated early in my childhood, and—unconventionally—chose to separate my brother and me: He went to live with our mother, while I lived with our father. He was an artist, so I grew up surrounded by creativity and the intoxicating pull of artistic passion. Yet, with that beauty came a certain degree of instability. We lived in many different places and, at times, in a collective with other families., I learned at an early age to care for myself, but I also learned to relate to and trust people from different backgrounds and parts of the world, as we had a constant flow of people coming in and out of our lives throughout my childhood. Looking back, it may have seemed chaotic from the outside—unstable and insecure—but I remember it as a childhood full of freedom.

While my home life lacked structure, I found grounding in gymnastics—a discipline that demanded both individual excellence and team collaboration. I loved the self-control, the predictability, and the mutual reliance among my fellow gymnasts. For years, gymnastics was the cornerstone of my identity.

But at 15 years old, everything changed.

A serious back injury ended my days as a gymnast almost overnight. It was my first major life challenge, bringing not only physical limitations but a loss of identity. Suddenly, I was no longer "the gymnast." The following few years were marked by confusion and self-exploration, as I tried to understand who I was beyond what I had once been.

By 17, I left Denmark for London in search of answers and freedom, only to return home a year later still uncertain of my path. When I began an academic bridging program, I carried with me values my parents instilled: from my creative father, fearlessness—"You can do anything if you put your mind to it." From my schoolteacher mother, precision—"Whatever you choose, do it with excellence so you don't waste your time."

In the midst of figuring out my path, my back injury continued to interfere with my life. Since I was struggling physically, I never knew if I could make it to my class, so I enrolled in multiple courses instead of just one. While managing my chronic back issues, doctors eventually discovered a rare anatomical anomaly—an extra vertebra—that likely contributed to my recurring injuries. Despite the physical setbacks, I kept moving forward.

In the mid-1990s, I finally decided to get a university degree and enrolled at the Royal School of Library and Information Science—not because I wanted to be a librarian, but because I felt an urgent need to do something with my life. To my surprise, that half-hearted step into academia became an opportunity to develop new skills. The structure and discipline these studies required from me suited me surprisingly well. I could argue that this was where I discovered my early passion for digital communication and technology.

After graduating, a friend of my then-husband recommended me for a User Interface Designer role at Nokia, a global technology company with 60,000 employees. I had little idea what I was stepping into—or if I was qualified—but I interviewed and got the job. Just eight months later, I was promoted to team lead.

Over the next twelve years, I held increasingly senior roles, eventually managing a department of over 200 people. I was selected for a high-potential talent program, which gave me access to global business education, including two executive courses at London Business School—one in strategy and the other in leading change.

Through these jobs I was given a lot of travel opportunities around the world. We conducted field research to better understand consumer needs and develop more relevant products, and I embraced every opportunity and challenge that was thrown at me. But as I grew professionally, my personal life became more complex. I worked in Finland but lived in Copenhagen, co-parenting my young son from my first marriage while raising my baby daughter with my current partner. My weekly commute—Monday through Thursday in Finland, Friday through Sunday in Denmark—was demanding. Despite a lot of support from my partner, I was stretched thin and, perhaps more painfully, judged harshly by other women who had chosen to be stay-at-home moms. Their criticism stung, but ultimately led me to reevaluate my circle and prioritize relationships that honored my choices as a working mother.

I eventually moved to a company in Denmark, stepping into my next executive role as Vice President of a highly male-dominated tech firm—heading a small business unit and, for the first time, carrying full P&L responsibility. This was also the company where I met Andreas—a young, talented leader who, even then, saw not gender, but equality. The culture in this company was markedly different from what I had experienced in the past. I was used to being the only female leader in leadership teams. However, I wasn't used to gender discrimination. This new company was political, exclusionary, and often hostile to female leadership. I was repeatedly talked over in meetings, excluded from informal power spaces like golf outings and business dinners, *and became the subject of behind-the-scenes scrutiny. In response, I changed. I became louder, more assertive, and sharper at the edges—traits I had never needed or wanted to cultivate, but felt I had to in order to survive in that culture.*

The abrupt shifts made me doubt myself. It felt like I'd gone from fearless leader to fearful little girl. The emotional toll it took on me was enormous. I gained weight. I lost joy. I didn't know who I could trust or who I could talk to.

Honestly, I stayed in that position two years too long—out of stubbornness, pride, and a belief that walking away was akin to failure. In the end, the company let me go—and it turned out to be the best thing that could have happened. I took four months off work and hired a coach to reflect, recover, and rebuild. During that time, I realized I had lost myself trying to survive in an environment where I was never meant to thrive. And that experience ultimately reshaped how I evaluate work cultures, how I lead others, and how I protect my well-being.

In the years that followed, I reclaimed myself and chose roles that aligned with my values. For example, I took a step down, accepting a position at a mission-driven company in the hearing aid industry, even when I had offers for bigger roles with higher salaries at larger corporations. For me, cultural fit mattered more than the money. The company's environment was healthy, inclusive, and collaborative. I flourished—rediscovering my voice and becoming the leader I always wanted to be: someone who was empathetic, strategic, and unapologetically myself.

Today, life is good, and I am as settled as I'll ever be—in who I am as a professional, a mother, and a partner. I serve as a Senior Vice President at my company, live north of Copenhagen, and am in my early fifties. My daughter is still at home, and my son has recently moved out. Not long ago, I had an eye-opening conversation with my daughter. I'd been invited to join a board but hesitated, wondering if I was being asked only to fill a diversity quota. When we talked about it, my daughter challenged me: "Even if that's true, Mom. If not you... then who? And will they fight for the right things, the way that you will?" Her wisdom reminded me why representation matters, and I proudly accepted the role.

Leadership, I've learned, is an ever-evolving journey, and I'm still growing. I often tell my male manager, "If you notice I haven't spoken up in a while, give me a nudge." He's aware of my past positions and how important it is to me that I use my voice. And to be clear, using my voice doesn't mean being the loudest. It means having the courage to speak my truth while also creating spaces for others to do the same.

Currently, I'm mentoring more people than ever before—both women and men, intentionally. Why? Because gender equity will never be achieved in separation; it can only be achieved through collaboration. And, quite frankly, there are things both genders need to do differently.

So, to the next generation of male leaders: Listen when women speak. Understand that female passion is not irrationality—it's conviction. Don't mistake emotional expression for a lack of competence. Women's voices bring a dimension to leadership that benefits the entire organization.

And, to the next generation of female leaders: Lean in and speak up. Don't wait to be invited into the conversation—create space for yourself and others. Read the room. Channel your passion strategically, but never diminish it. Most importantly, don't confine yourself to all-female spaces. Yes, women must support women—but we must also engage men as allies. We must step into integrated environments and challenge the status quo, not simply echo our frustrations in safe spaces.

For all of us, this change will require courage, honesty, and unity. So I leave you with this: No matter who you are or what your gender is, never lose yourself in the pursuit of success. If you do lose yourself—pause, recalibrate, and return to who you truly are. Advocate not just for yourself, not just for women, but for all who seek to lead with integrity. Why? Because someday, sooner than we'd like to admit, the next generation will inherit the legacy we've built. What kind of legacy do you want to leave behind? Let it include equality and inclusion. Let it be worthy of those who come after us.

As you've read, Janne's leadership ethos has never been about ascending only with women; it's been about empowering everyone to rise alongside her. We can all benefit from mirroring her mindset in our own careers and organizations.

Activities for Overcoming Gender Discrepancies in the Workplace

Despite cultural progress, we're still far from where we need to be. Women continue to be underrepresented in leadership, undervalued in compensation, and underestimated in capability. But these barriers are not immovable. As leaders—regardless of gender—we have both the responsibility and the power to challenge these norms and close the gender gap.

It's time to take action because inclusion shouldn't be a side project. Do the following activities and don't move on to the next chapter until you've done them.

#1: It Starts at Home:

If you have children, teach your daughters and sons these lessons. Teach them they are equals and to stand up for themselves and each other. Ask yourself: Do I want my daughter living with the glass ceiling? Let that question push you to act.

#2: Stand Up for Yourself:

If someone is treating you unfairly because of your gender, call it out. Be assertive. Stand up for yourself. Hold your stance with confidence. Involve your manager or HR if you have to.

#3: Support Other Women:

Just as you stand up for yourself, you should stand up for other women when they are faced with gender-based discrimination. Women who *stand together* have the best chance at overcoming unfair gender-driven systems.

#4: Reject Assimilation:

Women don't need to be like men to lead effectively, so don't masculinize yourself to gain entry into the boys' club. Instead, stay true to who you are. Build your own circle of influence. Find the environments that fit your style. Join peer councils, women's leadership groups, or masterminds that fuel your confidence and expand your visibility.

#5: Reflection Exercise:

Whether you're a parent or not, write a letter to your daughter, a young girl who needs someone like you to believe in her and advocate for her. What are your actions teaching her and the next generation? Are you reinforcing gender gaps, or working to close them? Are you building a future she can thrive in?

Call to Action for Leaders

After reading this chapter, you should feel an urgent push to act. If you don't, you are part of the problem in today's business world. I understand that if you're from the U.S., you may be at a disadvantage in recognizing just how drastic the gender biases are—and how inaccurate the gender narratives remain—in this country. (As an immigrant, I'm still shocked by what I see in mainstream U.S. news, even after being in this country for over a decade!) Remember way back in Chapter 1 when I mentioned the Global Gender Gap report? Sweden ranks fifth in the world, while the U.S. ranks forty-third (Ruggeri, 2023). It's time to address these biases and outdated narratives and stop living in denial. Make sure you are doing the following.

#1: It Starts at Home:

Teach your daughters and sons these lessons. If you don't have children, then to your nieces, nephews, etc. Teach girls and boys that they are equal and teach them to stand up for themselves and others at school. Do you really want the next generation of women to live with the glass ceiling? This question should kick you into gear to start addressing this in your own organization.

#2: Create Inclusive Environments:

Speak up when something feels wrong. Don't let blurred lines go unchecked. Invite a woman to sit beside you. Alter the seating arrangements in a meeting. Vary who gets addressed first. Inclusion starts with intention.

#3: Break the Glass Ceiling:

As mentioned earlier, there are three clear ways leaders can break the glass ceiling: sponsorship, addressing unconscious bias, and promoting women. Start taking these actions today.

#4: Don't Just Match—Pay What the Role Is Worth:

If you're hiring for a role, set the salary based on the value of the position—and don't adjust it depending on the gender of the person applying. This is how we begin to correct deeply ingrained systemic imbalances. Women have been historically underpaid and often ask for less than a role is budgeted for. So don't be cheap. Pay women what the role is worth—the same as you would a man. (It's baffling that I even have to state this.)

#5: Create Talent Programs:

Identify the women who have the utmost leadership potential. Even if they are young or new to the company, that's okay. Create a talent program and start working with them one to two years early to fine-tune and develop their skills. This gives them the best chance at breaking the glass ceiling in their careers. (And be sure to balance the talent pool fairly! Don't just include one woman and have nine men. Make it five and five.)

Scan this QR code to check out more resources.

Quick Pause — Has this book been impactful?

If this book moved you, challenged you, or gave you something to carry forward, I assume you've already left a review on Amazon. I'd like to extend my gratitude and appreciation for your kind gesture. Thank you for supporting my work and for sharing how it impacted you. Your review has helped, and will continue to help, this book reach women who are standing where you once stood: on the edge of self-doubt, ready for more, or searching for something to light the way. Maybe your review has already become the very reason someone took a chance on this book and themselves.

And if you haven't yet—would you consider leaving a review on Amazon? I know it's easy to assume someone else will or that your one review won't make a difference, but your voice genuinely matters. Reviews are often the reason someone picks up a book (or decides to *not* pick up a book). Whether it's one sentence or several, your words can be part of the ripple effect. Just scan the QR code below to leave a review on Amazon. Thank you for showing up—not just for your own transformation, but for others' transformations as well.

You're a true diamond, helping to rewrite the story of what's possible. Now, the book isn't over yet, so read on to unlock your full potential.

Chapter 13: Empowering the Next Generation of Female Leaders

"The emerging woman... will be strong-minded, strong-hearted, strong-souled, and strong-bodied... strength and beauty must go together."
— Louisa May Alcott

As mentioned earlier, the underrepresentation of women in senior leadership remains a persistent and critical concern in the business world. Though strides have been made toward gender parity, many aspiring women still look upward and don't see themselves reflected in positions of influence. Without that visibility, the path to leadership can feel uncertain, ambiguous, or even unattainable. This reinforces internalized narratives like impostor syndrome, discouraging women from self-advocating and further entrenching existing systems.

It reminds me of the age-old question: "What came first: the chicken or the egg?" There had to be an egg for a chicken to be born. And yet, there had to be a chicken to fertilize an egg. Without ever reaching an answer, we continue to stumble between the two. In this context, the question becomes: "What came first—women rising or men giving women opportunities?" Women must rise for men to give them opportunities—yet men must give women opportunities for them to rise. We could continue to circle this question—and never come to an answer—or both genders can start taking action now. (The U.S. would try to make this topic political, but this isn't political. If anyone has a problem with this, go read another book—oh wait, you're in the final chapter.)

By working together, we can undergo an imperative paradigm shift—one that invites us to not merely adapt within existing frameworks, but to remodel them altogether. All leaders—male and female—must equip women with the tools to seize more opportunities. And once women gain a seat at the table, they—and their male allies— must lift other women as well. Because if we are not extending a hand to others as we climb, then what is the point of our progress?

This forward-looking chapter serves as a blueprint for preparing, elevating, and empowering the emerging generation to reimagine and redefine today's professional climate. We'll reflect on legacy-building and the transformational impact of mentorship and sponsorship. Plus, we'll hear from two women, Carolina and Ryanna. Carolina is a Latina CEO in a male-dominated industry, whose leadership not only broke the glass ceiling but created pathways for the next generation of women. Ryanna is a rising professional whose trajectory was accelerated by someone believing in her. Their stories together underscore a fundamental truth: Leadership is not about hoarding power but distributing it.

Building a Legacy of Leadership

By now, you understand the foundational elements of building a lasting leadership legacy (hint: everything we've discussed so far): a clear understanding of your values, an authentic presence, and the courage to hold true to those values. It's being grounded in self-mastery that you become better equipped to influence organizational culture.

A critical component of this legacy is female-to-female mentorship. This form of guidance uniquely addresses the gender-specific challenges women often face in professional environments: navigating power dynamics, negotiating compensation, owning your femininity, etc. Experienced female mentors offer advice and validation, reminding rising females they are not alone and are unequivocally capable.

As discussed in Chapter 12: Overcoming Gender Discrepancies in the Workplace, mentorship alone isn't sufficient, though. Think of it like this: Mentorship nurtures growth, but sponsorship accelerates advancement. Sponsors advocate for you when you're not in the room. They also facilitate introductions and use their influence to open doors that will elevate your career.

Together, mentorship and sponsorship create spaces for capable women to lead, shatter the glass ceiling for themselves and for countless others who follow, and amplify their legacy even further.

Carolina's Story: Feminine, Fearless, and Breaking Cycles

Few stories better illustrate what's possible for women in the future than Carolina's. A cofounder and CEO of a luxury painting company, she leads a mostly male team with composure, precision, and unshakeable authority. As one of a few women—and even fewer Latina women—leading in her industry, Carolina is more than a role model. She's a trailblazer.

> *I was born in Mexico City and immigrated to the United States at the age of eight, following a defining moment in my family's story. My mother had made up her mind—she was done living in survival mode and was determined to create a better life for herself and me. She gave my father a choice: Stay in Mexico and continue his destructive cycle with alcohol, or come with us and start over. He chose to come—but this journey, this transformation, was one my mother had already decided on. That's the kind of warrior she is—and the kind she raised me to be.*
>
> *I adapted quickly to a new environment and culture. Within a year, I had learned English, and in fourth grade, I discovered something deeper: a burning drive to excel. A local grocery store launched a contest where students wrote essays about their favorite teacher and collected receipts. I became obsessed with winning—asking strangers for receipts and even digging through the store's trash cans after dark for the discarded ones. I submitted my essay with thousands of receipts—and won. The prize went to my school, my teacher, and my class. But what I truly won was the realization that with relentless*

focus and resourcefulness, I could accomplish anything.

But the path wasn't linear. My father relapsed into alcoholism a few years after we arrived in the U.S. By my late teens, my parents divorced. It was painful and eye-opening. While my father taught me valuable lessons—about sales, resilience, and charm—he also taught me the hardest lesson: Disappointment stems from unmet expectations. Eventually, I stopped expecting anything from him. I was done letting his decisions get to me or get in the way.

My mother, on the other hand, was (and is) my real-life hero. She had already endured the unimaginable. Not only with him, but with losing two newborn daughters, each just days old. I am her only living daughter, so she poured all her love, hope, and strength into raising me with grace and fire.

At 17, I graduated from high school early and started my first business—a balloon decorating company. At the same time, I was working as a bookkeeper for local house painters, including Louis—one of the best painters in town, no doubt. For thirty-four years, he's honed his craft with dedication and excellence. What he was missing wasn't skill, but support. That's where I came in. I became the fuel for his operation and learned countless lessons from him. Our bond grew deeper than that of just business partners. In many ways, the emotional connection we've built is stronger than the one I share with my biological father.

Those early career years taught me grit. I also began to see a dangerous pattern forming in my own life—dabbling in alcohol, surrounded by chaos, repeating cycles I'd promised myself I would break. So I made a choice. I told my then-boyfriend my habits were changing. He chose to change too. That man became my husband of fifteen years and father to our three children. Together, we embraced a sober lifestyle and made deep, transformative changes when we joined The Church of Jesus Christ of Latter-day Saints.

By the time I was pregnant with my first, the balloon business died down. Meanwhile, I dove deeper into understanding the painting industry while working for Louis. At some point, he took an interest in my mother and asked for her number. Eventually, they married, and they've been together almost as long as my husband and I. Ironically, the man I saw as a father figure became my stepfather. The other partnering painter struggled with this change and ended up leaving the company to walk in a different direction. Louis and I restructured the business, and what followed was an astonishing transformation: We went from $400,000 in debt to building a thriving $6 million painting company.

Today, I serve as CEO and have done so for the past eighteen years, leading a team of about sixty employees—all of whom are currently men. About ten years back, I earned a BBA from the University of North Texas, becoming the first person in my mother's family to graduate from college. I learned a lot in my courses about business, but the greatest lessons didn't come from the classroom—they came from job sites, client meetings, and experience. I had to figure out for myself how to command respect in an industry where women—and female leaders—are rare.

Construction remains deeply male-dominated—and it's not a glamorous gig. Over the years, there have been a few female painters at our company—I'm always glad to have them—but it's a field that not many women enter or stay in (just like plumbing and HVAC). At any site, you'll typically find a male builder, a male superintendent, and male workers. Occasionally, a female homeowner or designer. And always me—often the only woman in the room. I've been talked over, ignored, patronized, and objectified. I've taken calls while pumping breast milk in my car. I've walked job sites while being openly ogled.

One experience I'll never forget involved a particularly difficult misogynistic client who belittled his wife and attempted to employ that same dominance over me. After our job with him was completed, he falsely accused our company of misapplying paint when, in truth, a section of his house had water damage. To maintain professionalism, we offered to touch up the affected area. Instead, he attempted to manipulate our painter into redoing much more and ordered him around like a pet. When I arrived on site and saw what had happened, I clarified that we had not agreed to those additional demands. The man erupted. I calmly responded, "OK. Have a wonderful day," and left with my employee. That moment solidified for me the importance of advocacy and boundaries, which I had learned from Louis early on. As he would say: Our workers break their backs for us, so we must have their backs at all times.

Establishing respect as a woman in leadership—particularly as a Latina mother of three—takes time, composure, and precision. Men in my field respect me not because I demanded it, but because I consistently led with integrity, clarity, and empathy. I listen before I speak—and I don't speak until I know with full certainty what needs to be said and what *decision serves the company best. So when I do speak, my employees pay attention.*

This confidence wasn't innate. It never is. Confidence is built through repetition. I used to struggle with difficult conversations, especially around termination. But like any skill, I practiced, rehearsed, roleplayed. And eventually, I mastered it. Now, I'm able to make those tough decisions with clarity and compassion—because I understand that avoiding them only builds what I call "emotional debt." The longer you delay addressing an issue, the more costly it becomes—just like financial debt. Putting it into monetary terms helped me grasp the importance of letting go of emotional baggage for good.

Despite my inner and outer accomplishments, I hit a plateau about two years ago. I felt stuck—not in a business crisis, but in a personal disconnect. I was no longer in love with my company. I knew I needed support, so I sought a business coach and hired Andreas.

He helped me begin a new chapter in business strategy and self-worth: I started giving myself credit for what I'd built. I began to uncover deeper emotional barriers that I didn't even know existed—like how, as a Hispanic woman raised in a working-class home, I'd unconsciously believed I didn't belong in the same rooms as my high-profile clients. I saw myself as a service provider, not a peer. Realizing this was pivotal. I began rewriting my inner narrative. I chose abundance over fear. I shifted my energy and began aligning with people who mirrored the future I wanted, rather than the past I had overcome. In doing all this work, I reconnected to my vision—not just for the company, but for the kind of leader and woman I wanted to be. Without doubt, the most meaningful outcome of this work is the example I now set for future generations and for my children—especially my daughter. She has been given a tangible vision that I never had growing up: a Latina mother as a CEO. That image alone will shape what she believes is possible for herself. Just recently, I noticed she was using the word "scared" frequently. (She's thirteen and grappling with those tender developmental years.) I gently encouraged her to swap "scared" for "challenging," "unknown," and "new." Instead of "This thing is scary," it becomes "This thing is unknown to me."—a simple shift in phrasing that turns fear into courage and curiosity. My hope is that she will learn to not let fear decide what she can or cannot do in this life.

And that is my hope for all young girls. I want to see more women in this industry if they want to be here. I don't want them thinking, "I can't do this because I'm female" or "because I'm a minority." So I'm breaking this cycle by starting an internship and mentorship program with seniors in high school from my alma mater, in hopes to attract more women into the field.

If I could change anything in my journey, it would only be this: I would have hired a coach sooner. No one hands you a blueprint to overcome impostor syndrome, to navigate gender dynamics, or to level up in your career and mindset simultaneously. But those tools exist and it's up to you to seek them out. And if you apply what you learn, those lessons can catapult you five years ahead. None of us are meant to live in comfort zones that stall growth. We are here to evolve and elevate.

My mother taught me that. She never stopped believing in the impossible. She never let life rob her of hope. After losing two daughters, she raised me with joy. After divorcing her husband, she wasn't cynical toward love. That resilience and faith defined our lives and became the compass for mine. So, whether you're navigating a boardroom, a job site, or the emotional wreckage of a generational pattern—know this: You can do anything you set your mind to. Absolutely. I've done it. And so can you.

The most inspiring part of Carolina's journey is how, generation after generation, the women in her family worked to create something better for those who came after them. Carolina's mom moved her family to the U.S. for better opportunities and left an unhealthy marriage. Carolina embraced those opportunities, began a sober life, and gave her daughter the awareness of feminine leadership. Now, as a teen, Carolina's daughter is rewriting internal narratives—gaining self-awareness and growth early, setting herself up for long-term success. (And imagine the impact this could one day have on her daughter if she has one!)

What Emerging Female Leaders Need to Succeed

Certain characteristics distinguish thriving female leaders from others. They're traits you'll recognize—ones we've returned to time and time again in this book: self-awareness, confidence, empathy, emotional intelligence, and resilience. These traits—each essential and teachable—should be at the forefront of every development conversation with rising female talent.

#1: Self-awareness (And Other "Self" Words):

This is always the starting point. You can't lead others with integrity or precision until you've learned and met yourself. This involves understanding your strengths, limitations, blind spots, and behavioral patterns—and then working through your not-so-good patterns to rise into a better version of yourself. Self-confidence, self-worth, self-esteem, and self-love—these are all vital to leading from a place of groundedness.

#2: Confidence:

It's essential to have a grounded belief in your abilities. And it doesn't have to look like cockiness or arrogance; it could look like trusting your own voice instead of waiting to be validated. Confidence is what encourages women to take calculated risks, assert their perspectives, and hold their ground—even in rooms where their presence is questioned or undervalued.

#3: Empathy:

This is one of the most strategic tools a leader can have. Empathy fosters trust and promotes psychological safety, which in turn builds high-performing teams rooted in mutual respect and authenticity.

#4: Emotional Intelligence (EQ):

EQ is the ability to recognize, regulate, and respond to emotions—both your own and others'. Leaders with high EQ can navigate complex situations with composure, knowing when to assert, when to listen, and when to pivot.

#5: Resilience:

In a world where women still face disproportionate scrutiny, this trait is indispensable. It allows you to endure setbacks, reframe adversity, and persevere through rejection. Those who are resilient tend to achieve more because, rather than crumbling, they rise stronger, more capable, and more determined.

It is our collective responsibility—regardless of gender or tenure—to cultivate, model, and reinforce these traits in our organizations.

Ryanna's Story: In Choosing Herself, She Was Chosen

Now let's shift perspective, from the view at the summit to the experience of someone still climbing, and what it means for them to be lent a hand.

POWER WITHOUT PERMISSION

Like many women, my life started with being a "good girl." My mother still jokes about how I would put myself to bed at just 1.5 years old. I would set my shoes nicely side-by-side next to the door and crawl into my crib with a bottle of milk. School was no different. I went into kindergarten knowing how to read, spell my name, and do math beyond my age level. I loved school so much that I never wanted to miss a single lesson. I strove for perfect attendance every year, some years earning an award for it among my peers.

Beyond my excellent attendance, I also excelled in school academically—though, in the American education system, that doesn't necessarily mean intelligence—just skill in memorization and following directions. I did my homework. I memorized material. I followed my teacher's orders. I aced every test. Repeat. Repeat. Repeat. And that's how I got straight A's (with the exception of a B+ here and there). I also never questioned authority, which bodes well in the American education system (and American society, for that matter). What adults said, went—and I simply obliged.

This system we're indoctrinated into also gives us a map for how our lives are supposed to be led. You go to school from age 5 to 18. You graduate with a high school diploma. You commit to a four-year college. You get a bachelor's degree. You continue your education or start your career. You work for thirty or more years. And then, you retire. I never questioned this model.

That is, until 2019, when I was 22 years old. I had recently graduated with a bachelor's degree in Psychology from UNC Asheville and moved back home to Southern California to start my post-college adult life. My dreams were lofty and naïve. "I will be a therapist! A researcher! Maybe I'll travel to another culture and conduct a psychological study!" Only... I couldn't do any of those things with just a BA.

One morning, sitting at the kitchen table in my parents' house, I perused various job listings and websites. Everything required a master's degree or a doctorate. What could I do with a BA in Psychology? Basically nothing. There was one occupation that had a plethora of openings on every job site though: behavior technician, utilizing ABA therapy to help children with autism or intellectual disabilities, whether at school or at home. I had worked and played with autistic children growing up and in school and always found love and laughter in their company, so I thought this might be a good fit for me. Plus, the starting salary for someone with a bachelor's degree was a whopping $19 per hour. I felt rich at the thought. While in college in North Carolina, I had various odd jobs that paid the minimum wage of $7.25 per hour, so this was a huge leap.

I applied to five companies and within days heard back from all five. At the time, I was surprised. But looking back, it's obvious why. For one, it's a field with an extremely high turnover rate. Second, people get hired for these positions with just a high school diploma. There's no other way to say it—I was a catch. A degree in psychology, a 3.84 GPA, extracurriculars like Division I Soccer and editor of a literary magazine, working three part-time jobs while in school. No... I was more than a catch; they were striking gold. And I was a young woman who had no idea of her worth.

I chose the company that seemed the most fitting, and everything was going well at first. The first few clients whose cases I worked on were young kids between ages four and twelve on the spectrum. It was fun. They were cute. And I was making more money than I had ever made in my life.

About three months into the job, my company told me they were assigning me to a new school case they had just received. I asked about the child I'd be working with and my supervisor's answers were a bit misleading. He was nine, and they were "still assessing him and couldn't say whether or not he had autism, but thought he did." I was confused, but I followed along, as any good girl who listens to authority would.

To make what could be a long story exceptionally shorter, I can tell you this: The child did not have autism. He had Oppositional Defiant Disorder (ODD). He verbally and physically bullied other kids. He often tried to stab me with scissors or threaten me with verbal insults. He would frequently stand on his desk, yell in the classroom, or roam around school. It wasn't the child's fault, though. He just came from an unfortunate home life: family members in prison, and an older brother and father in a local gang.

So, why do I share this? Because that tough experience is what gave me the brutal wake-up call I needed. My body was always on high alert and my nervous system was dysregulated nearly every single day. Sometimes I would come home with bruises. My Monday through Friday routine was rigorous and monotonous from 6:00 a.m. to 6:00 p.m. In short, I was... unhappy.

One evening, stuck in SoCal traffic around 6:30 p.m., it dawned on me that I was always out of the house before the sun rose and home after the sun had set. A question popped into my mind: "And I'm supposed to do this every week for at least thirty more years?" Suddenly, as if I were hit by a bolt of lightning, the life force within me jolted awake. More questions came: "What is all this for? Is this how I want to spend my time on Earth? What do I want to do? Who am I? What do I want out of life? What is my dream?" I had been such a robot to the system that this sudden burst of consciousness was overwhelming, and my mind spiraled.

That night, I struggled to go to sleep. So instead, I answered all the existential questions that I felt I should have asked myself years earlier. My ultimate goal was, well, to do whatever the hell I wanted. To not waste my time on Earth doing things I didn't want to do or get told by others what to do. I wanted to be my own authority. To travel. To write. To eventually start my own business, helping those who struggle with mental health (since I was on the tail end of a long journey battling depression, anxiety, anorexia, bulimia, binge eating disorder, and suicidal ideation that began in my teen years). Suddenly, with this new vision, I was determined to create my life on my terms. The truth is, you have to work hard no matter what, so you can either work hard for somebody else's dream or for your own. Now that I knew mine, I was going to choose it... Every. Single. Time. I put in my two-week notice and from then on focused on bringing my passions to life.

Which brings me to today. It's been six years since that awakening. Now, I'm 28 years old and pregnant with my first child. The transition from my early- to late-twenties has been wild, spontaneous, and amazing, to say the least. I brought so many of my dreams to life. I have published seven books—six poetry collections and one novel. I obtained a Master of Fine Arts Degree in Creative Writing with a 4.0 GPA. I solo traveled to more than one-third of the

U.S. national parks. And there were countless times I felt immense gratitude for who I was and the life I was living. On a random Tuesday morning, I was hiking an 8,000 foot mountain or sitting in a hot spring letting little fish clean my feet while many across the country were stuck in jobs they hated or in unconscious, robot-like lifestyles.

 As beautiful, life-giving, and wisdom-filled as my journey has been though, it hasn't all been glamorous. There were times I had $300 to my name and I had no idea where my next bout of money was coming from. For one and a half months straight, in fact, I did "van life" in my Volkswagen Jetta, staying at free BLM (Bureau of Land Management) campsites, because that's what I could afford. There were times I desperately needed money and would pick up Uber Eats or Instacart shifts in random states so I'd have enough for bills, food, and gas—all while working more than eighty hours a week writing books and marketing my work with virtually no pay, in an attempt to bring my passions to life. Yet, I remained resilient, knowing deep down to stay the course and trust what I was doing.

 And in 2024, it all paid off. I started hosting my own open mic events and women's mental health journaling workshops. I started my own lifestyle brand, podcast, and publishing company—All With Heart. I started doing freelance work: copy editing, book formatting, blog writing, and ghostwriting. And, for the first time in my entrepreneurial journey, I began to see consistent money from doing what I loved.

 It was during this time that I met Andreas. He'd told a social media management company he needed a writer, and my friend—who worked there—passed along my contact information. We hopped on *a call, and the first thing he said was, "I don't want to hear fluff. I don't want to hear your résumé. I want to hear who you are." I already knew I liked his character. I shared with him, for the most part, everything I've just shared with you now. "You're interesting," he said. "I'm going to give you one writing project and see how you do."*

That one writing project turned into many and eventually became, "Ryanna, English is my second language, so I'd like your help with my book for businesswomen. Also, I'd like to find a way to incorporate you into the book so I can help elevate you and get your name out there." Count me in—without hesitation.

Do you know the kind of confidence and life that brings to a young woman who, up until that point—besides her own family and friends—was the only one who believed in her? Now, someone from the generation above me was not only hiring me for a long-term writing project, but also involving me so I could gain exposure. Imagine my shock when he told me his life story and I realized that people like me were part of his life's purpose to help. He could have hired a seasoned fifty-something who'd been in the ghostwriting world for decades. But instead, he chose... me. A woman sub-thirty, pregnant with her first child, waiting for someone other than herself to see her worth.

I hope this further cements and proves all the many things Andreas has taught and discussed in this book. He is not a man who talks the talk—he actually walks it, with passion, intelligence, and open-mindedness.

And, as for my personal story, I'd like to leave you with this: Your current life is not in the hands of someone else—it is due to a culmination of

> *decisions you've made. So if there are things you don't like, change them. If there's toxicity, remove it. If you need to grow and take a hard look at yourself, do it. As far as you know, you only have one life. How do you want to spend your eighty or so years here? Don't waste them. Find the courage to step out and follow your dreams, even if at first nobody believes in you. Because eventually, someone will. Then someone else. And so on. Your dreams can absolutely become your reality if you take tangible steps toward them every day.*

Ryanna—a young professional, creative, and entrepreneur—like many in her generation, didn't yet have the titles, experience, or proof. Her story reminds us of two things: the importance of believing in yourself and the importance of believing in others. For seasoned leaders, remember that believing in someone young can be *the spark that ignites an entire career.*

Activities for Empowering the Next Generation of Female Leaders

Former U.S. Secretary of State Madeleine Albright once stated, "There's a special place in hell for women who don't help each other." The opposite is also true—when one rises, the path becomes easier for all. So cultivate environments where women amplify each other's voices, advocate in rooms of influence, and remove competition from the equation once and for all.

And men—this applies to you too. "There's a special place in hell for men who don't help women," and, likewise, a special place in business for those who do. If your executive team mirrors only your own demographic, you're part of the problem, and it's time to change that.

Take the following steps so that you are building the kind of world you'd be proud to leave behind. Don't move on to the next chapter until you've done them.

#1: Leadership Reflection:

Ask yourself: How am I paying it forward? What structures am I building to ensure diverse leadership? What legacy am I actively shaping?

#2: Build a Legacy Checklist:

These actions won't be completed overnight. Begin with one and commit to progress.

- Sponsor at least one woman beyond your immediate network.
- Establish or participate in a mentorship program within your organization.
- Audit your leadership team's diversity—who is missing from the table?
- Commit to promoting women, celebrating their wins publicly, and paying them higher salaries.
- Integrate leadership development into your organization.
- Let them be brilliant!

#3: Start a Conversation with Men:

Don't attack them—that won't make men listen. Instead, help them understand. Speak with them about the topics in this book. Ask them: "Do you have a program in your company that helps get more women involved as leaders?"

#4: Take on a Mentee:

By this point in the book, if you've been implementing the lessons and activities, you have the skills of a true leader. (Don't give me any impostor syndrome about this!) As a leader, it's time to start sharing your wisdom and guidance with others. Mentor a younger, rising female in your organization. Lend this book to them.

#5: Don't Stagnate:

Continue your ongoing growth. The work doesn't end just because we've reached the final chapter. Join our online community. (Hell, give another woman your login info!) For purchasing this book, you can get free access to the community. Listen to my podcast. Check out the articles and ebooks on my website, or my favorite resources that have nothing to do with me and my business.

Call to Action for Leaders

Leaders—it's on you to put this into action. As people who are the head of teams or organizations, you hold the key to influence and power. Don't be the leader who keeps the world exactly the same. Be the leader who stands out, speaks up, and makes changes—not only for the betterment of your organization, but for women, for men, and for the future of humanity. Make sure you are doing the following:

#1: Promote Representation:

If your team or company does not have diverse representation, especially at decision-making levels, then you need to rethink how you recruit, promote, and mentor. Take what you learn and create more inclusion.

#2: Champion Women:

No matter your gender, stop perpetuating harmful narratives against women in power. Uplift women, especially those who are breaking into spaces that have historically excluded them. And if you're a woman who's offered a position—even if it feels like tokenism—say yes. That's how you can drive change and open the door for even more women.

#3: SHE Counsel Adjustment:

If you have a SHE Counsel or employees in a SHE Counsel, make sure that the space is not an echo chamber. Invite men to come to the group as either listeners or guest speakers.

#4: Mentor and Sponsor:

If you haven't already taken the steps to mentor or sponsor anyone from previous chapter callouts, now is the time to take action. Commit to mentoring or sponsoring one woman in the next six months. Why? Because women are capable, needed in leadership, and deserve the chance to break the glass ceiling. And female leaders, remember: There is room for more than one of you at the table, and this is your chance to give back to someone who is walking in shoes you once walked in yourself.

#5: Don't Stagnate Just Because You Are a Leader Already:

This work doesn't end with the final chapter—or with your leadership title. Keep growing. Listen to my podcast. Check out some of the blog posts and ebooks on my website. Join my *Power Without Permission* community. (You can even give someone else your login info!) It has mini courses, videos, mentors (including myself), guest speakers, and countless tools to help you with impostor syndrome and the other topics in this book. If you purchased this book, it's completely free for you.

Just scan this QR code to get started.

Section V: Unlock Your Full Potential

Conclusion

Although our time together in these pages is coming to an end, your journey is far from over. In fact, if you've engaged deeply with the reflections, exercises, and insights shared throughout this book, then you're already a brilliant diamond—refined, resilient, and shining. This is only the beginning of what can be an extraordinary, intentional, and fulfilling future.

When we commit to evolving—both personally and professionally—we inevitably invite success, meaning, and impact into our lives. Remember: You don't have to be perfect, you just have to be committed to growth, which will require you to **ADAPT**. The world will shift around you—sometimes gently, sometimes with force—and your ability to stay grounded in who you are while navigating those shifts will define your trajectory. So, stay **Aware** of your inner world—your strengths, your shadows, and your unique brilliance. Walk with intention in the **Direction** of your vision, and when the path shifts, have the courage to take **Action** and pivot. This is how clarity emerges. This is how **Purpose** is revealed. And when you live with purpose, your **Transformation** extends beyond yourself, igniting transformation in others as well.

If there is one message I hope lingers with you, it's this: There is no singular mold for what a leader should look or sound like. The most effective leaders are not the loudest in the room, nor the ones who lead by fear or force. They lead from within—anchored in self-awareness, guided by empathy, powered by resilience, and committed to lifting others as they rise. These are the women whose stories you've encountered throughout this book.

So, disarm your impostor syndrome with grit and grace like Martha. Master your identity like Julie. Carry emotional intelligence into every room like Michele. Face your fears and show up—again and again—like Kana. Navigate power dynamics with unwavering strength like Cheryl. Know your worth inside and outside of the office like Stephanie. Build and lean on your network through the inevitable ebbs and flows like Cindy. Take bold action, no matter the circumstance, like

Marlene. Command space with quiet confidence like Marina. Lead with vision and an unshakable sense of purpose like Alyssa. Challenge gender norms with both strength and softness like Janne. Pave the way for the next generation like Carolina. And finally, recognize the diamonds in the rough from a younger generation, like Ryanna, and help them rise.

There's a Swedish concept called *lagom*, which roughly translates to "just enough." Unlike the relentless pursuit of the so-called American Dream, *lagom* speaks to a life of balance, contentment, and service. Remember when I shared my story with you, and I recalled a moment from my childhood, when my mother and I—despite living with very little—went out to collect donations for the Red Cross? When I asked why we didn't keep the money for ourselves, my mother looked at me as though the very question was absurd. We had dinner—even if it was only instant noodles—and others out there had even less. That was my first understanding of *lagom*. We had enough—and that meant it was time to help others. You've read this book, heard the stories, done the work, and gathered new knowledge. Now you have enough. This is your *lagom* and it's time to give to others. Time to mentor. To lead by example. To create space for others to grow.

To the men who read this book from start to finish: You are allies in this work, and your leadership is vital. May the insights you've gained here inspire you to advocate for and champion the women around you—your colleagues, your partners, your future daughters—and yes, your mothers. The women who raised you, who taught you, who shaped you. The very women who made your ability to read this book possible.

This book would not exist without my mother. Her life, sacrifices, and dignity in the face of limitation inspired everything you've just read. She recently turned eighty years old, and I can tell you she deserved more than this world gave her— yet somehow, she's always remained grateful, grounded, and generous. She never asked for more, and somehow she gave me everything. This book is for her—and it is also for you.

To every woman reading this: You deserve better, just like my mother. You deserve equity. You deserve leadership. You deserve a chance. You deserve the right to exist freely, without scrutiny or shame, whether you choose to build a career, raise a family, or do both. You deserve to take up space, to be seen, and to be heard.

As we continue to grow individually and collectively, my final request is simple: Always know that you are powerful and you don't need anybody's permission. Live this wisdom and these lessons. Share what you've learned with five women. That's how we spark a ripple effect—human to human, woman to woman, leader to leader—that can change the world one person at a time.

So, What's Next?

You came to this book seeking development both personally and professionally. Through these lessons, stories, and activities, you have elevated yourself, hopefully moving from the aspiring zone to the thriving zone on the Leadership Awareness Ladder, and learned to ADAPT as a leader—cultivating Awareness, Direction, Action, Purpose, and Transformation).

So… what's next? Well, as I've mentioned before, your journey doesn't end here. Growth is a lifelong process, and the moment we stop pursuing it, we plateau. You don't have to go it alone, either. If this book has resonated with you and you've transformed yourself through it, I encourage you to explore my podcast, blog posts, and ebooks, and reach out to any of the co-authors whose stories inspired you. Also, you can join my online community, where you can grow alongside like-minded female entrepreneurs, businesswomen, and men who support gender equality. It is free for you since you purchased this book. Just scan the QR code below to get started.

Meet The Authors

Martha Chrisander A former journalist turned marketing leader, Martha has never lost her love for a good story. (Fun fact: She once wrote an article for Playboy about the bar scene at her alma mater, UIUC.) She's a dual American–Swedish citizen, living in Malmö, Sweden, and spends most of her time courtside with her husband—watching their two basketball-obsessed boys sink shots—or digging into leadership, cybersecurity, and storytelling for tech brands. With more than 15 years of experience in B2B SaaS marketing, Martha specializes in turning complex information into messaging that connects. She's always up for exploring fascinating people and ideas. You can connect with her on LinkedIn, where she shares thoughts on leadership, marketing, and tech.

Julie Stone is a champion of human-centered business transformation with over two decades of experience turning empathy into action. As Director of Human Experience at Milestone Systems, she leads initiatives that integrate human insight into strategy, culture, and innovation. Her career began in sales, where her natural ability to listen deeply and build authentic connections quickly propelled her forward. Since then, she's mentored emerging leaders, driven customer experience programs, and initiated go-to-market transformations. She's always focused on what matters most: people. And is guided by a single truth: When we understand ourselves, we're better equipped to understand others. You can connect with her on LinkedIn.

Michele Jewett Growing up as a military kid among the last of the Baby Boomers, I learned early how to adapt, observe, and lead quietly. Today, I bring over 15 years of experience as an ICF-certified executive coach, former Director of HR, business owner, and longtime CEO facilitator. I specialize in transformational coaching for leaders and business owners, helping them align performance with fulfillment, build emotionally intelligent teams, and lead with both clarity and heart. Beyond the boardroom, I'm a mom to two phenomenal daughters who are each making a meaningful impact in the world. I'm a dedicated (and admittedly average) pickleball player, happiest with sand between my toes and salt air in my lungs. At 58, I was lucky enough to find an adventurous and loving husband, and together we've launched into what I call the most exciting chapter of life yet. It's all unfolding in just the way it should. You can connect with her on LinkedIn.

Kana Waanders is a Lead Senior Software Engineer with a passion for people and systems. From intern to team leader, she has built her career by blending technical excellence with empathetic leadership. She believes in cultivating growth by trusting others, embracing authenticity, and leading with compassion. Her journey is a testament to the power of overcoming fear and embracing vulnerability in leadership. Outside of tech, Kana brings energy and confidence to others as a certified Jazzercise instructor. Connect with her on LinkedIn.

Cheryl Strizelka has spent 41 years perfecting the art of reading the room, minding her own business, and staying hydrated. Her real credentials aren't her two decades in HR, her multiple college degrees, or her status as a wife and mother, but rather her finely tuned emotional intelligence, her uncanny ability to make people feel like they're the only person in the room, and her refreshingly modest opinion of her own flawlessness. She also cuts her own hair. You can connect with her on LinkedIn.

Stephanie Hammerwold is the head of HR at the Skirball Cultural Center in Los Angeles. Her HR experience includes warehousing, manufacturing, grocery, small business consulting, tech, and the arts. She is a member of ABC Collective, which is the DEI committee for the LA Chapter of the National Human Resources Association. When she is not immersed in the HR world, she volunteers her time with the California Coalition for Women Prisoners, where she is part of the prison visiting team, Writing Warriors' monthly meeting planning team, and hiring committee. In her free time, she can be found reading, baking, birdwatching, road-tripping, and training for her first marathon. Connect with her on LinkedIn and Instagram @roadtrip_and_me.

Cindy Chang is a seasoned product leader who thrives in ambiguity and leads with resilience, curiosity, and authenticity. Her early life taught her to face challenges head-on, build meaningful connections, and turn setbacks into strength. Those lessons became the muscle and scars she brings to scaling impactful products and building high-performing teams grounded in trust and accountability. Outside of work, she embraces her most important role as mom, seeing the world through her daughter's eyes and sharing a little Disney magic with the people she loves. You can connect with her on LinkedIn.

Marlene Braga has a wealth of experience in the arts, media, and television industries, having worked with prominent U.S. and international organizations such as Skirball Cultural Center, Woman on the Verge Productions, Azteca America, New York Women in Film & Television, A&E Television Networks, ABC News, and PBS. With a background in broadcast journalism and political science, Marlene has held roles such as Vice President, Public Programs, Agency Principal, Head of Programming-USA and Mexico, Director of Programming, Producer, and Production Associate. Marlene possesses considerable expertise in leading creative teams, overseeing TV program development, scriptwriting, video production, and large-scale live public events, as well as strategic planning for diverse public-facing entertainment programs. Marlene is "Made in Havana and born in Miami," a Cold War kid whose family fled the Cuban revolution in the early 1960s to settle in Florida. You can connect with her on LinkedIn.

Marina St. Cyr is a seasoned operational executive with over 20 years of experience leading business growth, strategic planning, and cross-functional teams. She currently serves as Senior Vice President for a portfolio of companies and commercial properties, while also advising high-growth firms like Mountain Group and RPT Products. Marina has helped scale companies from $14MM to $150MM in revenue, and has deep expertise in post-acquisition integration, ERP system implementation, and building sustainable operating models. Her leadership spans finance, legal, HR, sales ops, supply chain, and investor relations, and she is known for her strategic thinking, ethical leadership, and ability to execute. She holds a BS in Business Administration from USC and is completing her MBA at the Jack Welch Management Institute. She has also co-authored two books: *The New C-Suite* and *Cash Flowing Deals in Any Market*. You can connect with her on LinkedIn.

Alyssa Trenkamp With more than 20 years of marketing leadership experience in high-growth B2B SaaS companies, Alyssa has successfully navigated five company acquisitions, mastering the art of guiding teams through transformation while maintaining momentum and morale. Currently head of Americas Marketing for a global B2B technology company, Alyssa specializes in marketing that accelerates growth and drives B2B buyers to action. What sets her apart is her relationship-first approach to leadership—investing in people as true career capital and building networks that create lasting impact beyond any single role. She believes the corporate world needs leaders who can adapt without losing themselves. Connect with her on LinkedIn.

Janne Jakobsen is a results-oriented executive with over 25 years of international experience in business leadership, product and portfolio management, brand marketing, global marketing, and customer experience. Her leadership philosophy centers on customer focus, competitiveness, and strategic vision. As a generalist with a big-picture approach, Janne excels in leading through change and is passionate about creating the best solutions for both consumers and customers. This dedication to understanding target segments in depth has been a cornerstone of Janne's successful career. Through dedicated and personal leadership, Janne strives to build highly inclusive, dedicated, and passionate teams that foster collaboration and resilience. This approach has enabled companies, products, and businesses to realize their full potential. Connect with her on LinkedIn.

Carolina Hernandez is a Mexican-born entrepreneur, fund manager, real estate investor, and mother of three who has spent the last decade leading a multimillion-dollar painting company in one of the most male-dominated industries: construction. As the founder of Legacy Funds and co-founder of Louis Gloria Painting, she has helped families and business owners build lasting wealth through both craftsmanship and capital strategy. The first woman in her family to graduate from college, Carolina is passionate about helping women build lives of purpose, grit, and integrity. Through faith, resilience, and the power of self-reflection, she has redefined success on her own terms—and now teaches others to do the same. You can connect with her on LinkedIn.

Ryanna Hammond is a human being who is probably "being" just like you—with unique quirks, flaws, passions, and unanswered questions. She has a BA in Psychology and an MFA in Creative Writing from Emerson College. At just 28 years old, she has brought many of her dreams to life. She published six poetry collections and a contemporary multicultural romance novel titled *Searching For Emiliano*. She launched her own lifestyle brand and self-help podcast, *All With Heart*. And she started a side hustle helping others in need of writing services—whether that's copy editing, ghost writing, book formatting, or publishing coaching. In all that she does, her aim is to connect with others and help people feel less alone in this peculiar thing called human existence. You can learn more at www.allwithheart.com and connect with her on LinkedIn or Instagram @soulledwanderess.

Andreas Pettersson is an internationally experienced CEO, entrepreneur, and founder of Leaders ADAPT, LLC. With over 20 years of leading global business expansion, innovative product development, and strategic turnarounds (including six years building a successful startup), he's known for challenging the status quo and driving meaningful results. His ADAPT framework, CEO and executive masterminds, and one-on-one advisory programs help clients unleash their leadership brilliance and scale their businesses with confidence. He also shares insights on leadership, change, and resilience through real-world stories of challenge and transformation on his podcast *ADAPT or Die*. This is his first book. Learn more at www.leadersadapt.com and connect with him on LinkedIn or Instagram @andreastheceo.

Companion Discussion Guide

This guide was created with one central hope: that you won't journey through this book alone. While this book is about self-development as a person and professional, many of its ideas are meant to be tackled within a community—SHE Counsel, leadership circles, book clubs, accountability groups, a co-ed setting with male allies, or with colleagues and friends. No matter the setting, the goals are the same: to foster connection and brave conversations, to create powerful shifts in the community, and to help you go deeper into your own self-awareness, leadership presence, and personal legacy. There is no "correct" way to use this guide. Select a few questions to address during a session or tackle them one by one.

1. How has perfectionism, impostor syndrome, or insecure overachiever syndrome shown up in your career? What was the cost—mentally and energetically?
2. What internal narrative do you need to rewrite to grow into the next version of yourself?
3. What version of "success" were you taught to chase, and how has that definition evolved?
4. What does leading with emotional intelligence mean to you? How can it shift the culture around you?
5. How does the fear of judgment limit how you show up in your personal or professional life? What would change if that fear no longer held power over you?
6. How do you typically respond to power? Do you shrink, overcompensate, challenge, ignore, or navigate it strategically? What do you think shaped your current response to power?
7. What's one unspoken rule or political dynamic in your workplace? How do you learn this, and how do you navigate it today?
8. What is one professional boundary that you need to set but haven't yet? Why haven't you? What would it take for you to set it?
9. When you hear the word "networking," what comes up for you—excitement, discomfort, resistance? Why do

you think that is? Regardless of how it makes you feel, what's one step you could take today to deepen your current network?
10. What's one risk you've taken that changed your path for the better?
11. Where in your life or career are you still waiting to be chosen instead of choosing yourself?
12. Think of a woman you admire in your network or company. What is she modeling that you want to cultivate for yourself?
13. In what ways have you experienced or witnessed the boys' club in your workplace? How did it impact you or others?
14. Where do you see yourself conforming to outdated gender expectations? What would choosing yourself and your truth look like?
15. What biases do you think men in your industry hold about female leadership or women in general? How can you challenge this in conversation or with action?
16. What does "feminine leadership" mean to you? How is it misunderstood or undervalued in your industry?
17. What does being a confident, authentic leader look like for you, and how does it differ from how you've led in the past?
18. How can male allies more actively support gender equality?
19. What are you doing now to build your legacy? And how do you want people to remember you as a leader?
20. Who in your circle is part of the next generation of female leaders, and how can you actively invest in their growth? How can you create space for them at your table?

I hope this guide will be helpful in whatever circle of influence you bring its questions into.

POWER WITHOUT PERMISSION

For more resources, tips, and help, scan the QR code below.

Acknowledgements

Thank you to my mother, Karin Gustafsson (formerly Pettersson), for giving me the foundations for being a good human and making me the leader I am today. You taught me early to see people without judgment, to approach everyone with genuine curiosity, and to always give others a chance. You taught me that people go much further together than alone. You showed me how to forgive, move forward, and never go to bed angry so tomorrow wouldn't be ruined. You taught me that I can only be ashamed of myself and my own choices, never of others' expectations. You gave me the freedom to fail, to experiment, to make my own decisions, and to take responsibility for them. You've always seen further than I could, asking, "What happens next?" until I finally learned to see and grew into the successful visionary I am today. (Though it never mattered to you what my position was. "I don't give a damn if you become a street sweeper or a CEO," you said. "As long as you're happy.") As a parent, you adapted to who I was, not to some template of how children "should" be. And everything you gave me, I've had the joy of passing forward. Your wisdom lives through my leadership. Your love lives through my care for others. Your strength lives through my perseverance. Thank you, Mamma, for teaching me to live with an open heart, a strategic mind, and the courage to choose happiness. You never called yourself a leader, but you've always been one.

Thank you to my wife, Vesna Pettersson Fara, for believing in me, for pushing me to become a better version of myself every day, and for being my foundation—my forever rock and my forever wife. Honestly, there aren't enough words in both English and Swedish to describe how much you mean to me and our boys. You are strong, loving, and deeply empathic. You always make sure everyone is taken care of. You never fail to make me smile. You help me see things from a new perspective. You went above and beyond with Noel, making sure he got everything he needed and more, and I will never forget your strength during that time in our lives. Your amazing traits don't stop there. You're empathetic and open-minded. You're emotionally and socially intelligent. You're curious. You're ethical. You're business savvy. You juggle a lot—me, our boys, our real estate portfolio, our real estate fund, all our companies, investments, and so much more. You're also extremely resilient. You have the most insane willpower in the best way and just know how to make things work. In other words, you make life easy and amazing—and I love how well we work together. You are such an incredible, smart, brilliant, and powerful woman. Thank you for letting me pursue my passions. Thank you for your trust. Thank you for being my always and forever, and for being so authentically you.

Thank you to my sons, Leon, Noel, and Nelo. You three are the ultimate loves of my life—my inspiration, my why, my energy, my everything. You all can do anything you set your minds to. And you don't know it yet, but when you are prominent leaders, you will create space for more women than I have been able to at this point in my life.

Thank you to the incredible co-authors, ghost writer, editor, and publicist consultant who lent their time, stories, and wisdom to this book: Martha, Julie, Michele, Kana, Cheryl, Stephanie, Cindy, Marlene, Marina, Alyssa, Janne, Carolina, and Ryanna—thank you all for sharing your transformations so openly and brilliantly. You all mean so much to me. You are all such powerful, amazing, incredible, strong, courageous women. You helped make this book what it is. I will never forget this journey we've embarked on together and all the meetings, laughs, and text threads that came along with it. Ryanna, thank you for working so closely with me on this project as the ghost writer, since English is my second language. I'm sorry that you had to listen to hundreds of hours of videos and voice memos of my Swenglish (Swedish English). Marissa LaRocca, thank you for your time and dedication with editing the manuscript and fully seeing my passion for the topics covered in this book. Thank you Jennifer Jensen for all your guidance on publishing and promoting this book. And an extra thank you to Martha Chrisander. You continued to encourage me when I was struggling with getting this book across the finish line and did so much work related to the launch of this book and its community.

Thank you Marie Lood for being an early reader and reviewer, for offering your feedback, and for giving encouragement and ideas to elevate this book to the next level.

Thank you to Lars Thinggaard. You saw my brilliance before I did. You believed in me, opened doors for me, and gave me my first leadership mentor, Ole Stangegaard. Without you, I'm not sure this book would have been written until years from now. I will forever be grateful.

Thank you to Michael Madsen Sjo for amplifying who I already was and showing me who I could become. You helped me level up faster than I ever imagined. Your influence, and many of your lessons, live on in these pages. Thank you for being an amazing human being.

Thank you to the countless others who directly or indirectly supported or inspired me and this book, in no particular order: Marie Lood, Pär Åsfält, Beverly Wiesen, Lee Mehler, Leila Entezam, Norm Williams, Amit Kohtari, Bethany Laflam, Ken Hayes, Steve Shaw, Jeff Kunzelman, Paul Taylor, Cayla Craft, Ole Stangegaard, Sue Firth, Darren Rayner, Shionoya Shuichi (Shui), Brenda Jones, Isa Fidelino, Maja, Ingela, Soren, Rebecca, and anyone I've accidentally forgotten. Thank you all. (Whoever isn't listed, I'm really sorry. I will keep an updated list online for anyone who didn't appear in the published edition of this book.)

Finally, thank you to my current and future Leaders ADAPT clients. You can do anything you set your minds to, and never credit me for the work that you've done. You walked the journey yourself. You lived through the pain and experienced the gains. Your success stories are among my greatest joys. Remember to pay it forward. Mentor, uplift, and catalyze the next generation of strong female leaders and male allies.

References

Alongside my life experiences, the following works and software enriched the research, statistics, and frameworks in this book. I thank these authors, researchers, and organizations for their insights and inspiration.

American Association of University Women (AAUW). "Today's Gender Pay Gap Data Shows Decline in Progress Towards Equity." September 10, 2024. Retrieved from https://www.aauw.org/resources/news/media/press-releases/2024-gender-pay-gap-data/.

Anand, Varun. "The Five C's of Effective Communication in Project Management." EduHubSpot. January 13, 2025. Retrieved from https://www.eduhubspot.com/blogs/pmp/five-cs-of-effective-communication-in-project-management.

Anthropic. *Claude AI.* 2024. http://www.anthropic.com.

Anxiety & Depression Association of America. "Highlights: Workplace Stress and Anxiety Disorders Survey." 2006. Retrieved from https://adaa.org/workplace-stress-anxiety-disorders-survey.

Apollo Technical. "10 Surprising Statistics about Emotional Intelligence You Need to Know." February 4, 2025. Retrieved from https://www.apollotechnical.com/10-surprising-statistics-about-emotional-intelligence-you-need-to-know/.

Banks, Kerry. "The pull of procrastination." University Affairs. October 28, 2020. Retrieved from https://universityaffairs.ca/features/the-pull-of-procrastination/.

Bolden-Barrett, V. & Fecto, M. "Study: One-third of employers don't see how emotional intelligence is valuable to them." HR DIVE. August 19, 2019. Retrieved from https://www.hrdive.com/news/study-one-third-of-employers-dont-see-how-emotional-intelligence-is-valua/561036/.

Bradshaw, Ryan. "Networking Statistics." Apollo Technical. March 29, 2025. Retrieved from https://www.apollotechnical.com/networking-statistics/.

Dennison, Kara. "3 Ways To Be A More Inclusive Leader." Forbes. February 19, 2025. Retrieved from https://www.forbes.com/sites/karadennison/2025/02/19/3-ways-to-be-a-more-inclusive-leader/.

Dorsey, Keith. "From Glass Ceilings to Glass Cliffs: A Guide to Jumping, Not Falling." MIT Sloan Management Review. March 13, 2023. Retrieved from https://sloanreview.mit.edu/article/from-glass-ceilings-to-glass-cliffs-a-guide-to-jumping-not-falling/#:~:text=Some%20statistics%20suggest%20that%20the,delivered%20to%20your%20inbox%20monthly.

Ernst, Janae. "Are You Emotionally Intelligent? Here's How to Tell." Cornerstone University. June 5, 2017. Retrieved from https://www.cornerstone.edu/blog-post/are-you-emotionally-intelligent-heres-how-to-tell/.

Eurich, Tasha. "What Self-Awareness Really Is (And How to Cultivate It)." Harvard Business Review. January 4, 2018. Retrieved from https://hbr.org/2018/01/what-self-awareness-really-is-and-how-to-cultivate-i.

Eurich, Tasha. "Working with People Who Aren't Self-Aware." Harvard Business Review. October 19, 2018. Retrieved from https://hbr.org/2018/10/working-with-people-who-arent-self-aware.

Gino, Francesca. "Let Your Workers Rebel." Harvard Business Review. October– November 2016. Retrieved from https://www.hbs.edu/ris/Publication%20Files/Let%20your%20workers%20rebel_b87d0da9-de68-45be-a026-22dee862e6e4.pdf.

Goleman, Daniel. "The Four Domains of Emotional Intelligence." Big Think. December 11, 2024. Retrieved from https://www.youtube.com/watch?v=erfgEHHfFkU.

Grammarly Inc. *Grammarly*. 2024. http://www.grammarly.com.

Hawkins, D. R. *The Map of Consciousness Explained: A Proven Energy Scale to Actualize Your Ultimate Potential.* Hay House, 2020.

Koski, J., Xie, H. & Olson, I. "Understanding Social Hierarchies: The Neural and Psychological Foundations of Status Perception." National Library of Medicine. July 2, 2017. Retrieved from https://pmc.ncbi.nlm.nih.gov/articles/PMC5494206/.

Lean In. "Women in the Workplace." 2019. Retrieved from https://leanin.org/women-in-the-workplace/2019/glass-ceiling-and-the-broken-rung#.

Lencioni, P. *The Five Dysfunctions of a Team: A Leadership Fable.* Jossey-Bass, 2002.

Lowery, B. "Power and Influence." Stanford Graduate School of Business. 2018.

Martell, D. *Buy Back Your Time: Get Unstuck, Reclaim Your Freedom, and Build Your Empire.* Portfolio, 2023.

Marter, Joyce. "5 Types of Imposter Syndrome & How to Overcome Them." ChoosingTherapy.com. May 23, 2023. Retrieved from https://www.choosingtherapy.com/imposter-syndrometypes/#:~:text=The%20five%20imposter%20syndrome%20types,our%20ego%2C%20it%20is%20conquerable.&text=A%20Therapist%20Can%20Help%20You,the%20right%20therapist%20for%20you.

Masterson, M. *Ready, Fire, Aim: Zero to $100 Million in No Time Flat.* John Wiley & Sons Inc, 2008.

Mohr, Tara. "Why Women Don't Apply For Jobs Unless They're 100% Qualified." Harvard Business Review. August 25, 2014. Retrieved from https://hbr.org/2014/08/why-women-dont-apply-for-jobs-unless-theyre-100-qualified.

Novotney, Amy. "Procrastination or 'Intentional Delay?'" American Psychological Association (APA). January 2010. Retrieved from https://www.apa.org/gradpsych/2010/01/procrastination#:~:text=They%20to%20learn%20about%20the,did%20not%20take%20the%20course.

OpenAI. *ChatGPT.* 2024. http://openai.com/chatgpt.

Overvest, Marijn. "Negotation Statistics 2025 — 20 Key Figures." Procurement Tactics. February 18, 2025. Retrieved from https://procurementtactics.com/negotiation-statistics/.

Paulise, Luciana. "75% of Women Executives Experience Imposter Syndrome in the Workplace." Forbes. March 8, 2023. Retrieved from https://www.forbes.com/sites/lucianapaulise/2023/03/08/75-of-women-executives-experience-imposter-syndrome-in-the-workplace/.

Perret, C., Hart, E., & Powers, S. "From disorganized equality to efficient hierarchy: how group size drives the evolution of hierarchy in human societies." The Royal Society Publishing. June 3, 2020. Retrieved from https://royalsocietypublishing.org/doi/10.1098/rspb.2020.0693.

Pope, Carol. "82% of Full-Time Workers Who Asked for Pay Raise Got One." Lending Tree. November 18, 2024. Retrieved from https://www.lendingtree.com/debt-consolidation/pay-raisessurvey/#:~:text=Men%20are%20more%20likely%20to,also%20have%20a%20side%20hustle.

Robertson, D. *How to Think Like a Roman Emperor: The Stoic Philosophy of Marcus Aurelius.* St. Martin's Press, 2019.

Royal, Ken. "Who's Responsible for Employee Engagement." GALLUP. September 14, 2019. Retrieved from https://www.gallup.com/workplace/266822/engaged-employees-differently.aspx.

Ruggeri, Amanda. "The world's most gender-equal countries." BBC. September 27, 2023. Retrieved from https://www.bbc.com/travel/article/20230927-the-worlds- most-gender-equal-countries.

Salwender, M. & Stahlberg, D. "Do women only apply when they are 100% qualified, whereas men already apply when they are 60% qualified?" Wiley Online Library. September 1, 2024. Retrieved from https://onlinelibrary.wiley.com/doi/full/10.1002/ejsp.3109.

Smith, Katherine. "Mentoring in the Workplace: Examples and Best Practices." Boston College Center for Corporate Citizenship. January 19, 2024. Retrieved from https://ccc.bc.edu/content/ccc/blog-home/2024/01/mentoring-in-workplace-examples-best-practices.html.

Stillman, Jessica. "Brené Brown: This Is the No. 1 Skill You Need to Be a Great Leader Right Now." Inc. August 14, 2023. Retrieved from https://www.inc.com/jessica-stillman/brene-brown-calm-leadership-number-one-skill-post-pandemic.html.

Symon, Kerry. "Employees Thrive When Boundaries Are Respected. Here Are 6 Ways to Strengthen Boundaries Across Teams." Spring Health. November 7, 2024. Retrieved from https://www.springhealth.com/blog/6-ways-to-strengthen-boundaries-acrossteams#:~:text=Educate%20and%20empower%20employees,remote%20or%20hybrid%20work%20arrangements.

Thriving Center of Psychology. "Which Generation Struggles to Set Healthy Boundaries the Most?" October 28, 2022. Retrieved from https://thrivingcenterofpsych.com/blog/setting-healthy-boundaries/.

Ton, Jeffrey. "Networking: It's Not What You Think." Forbes. October 15, 2020. Retrieved from https://www.forbes.com/councils/forbestechcouncil/2020/10/15/networking-its-not-what-you-think/.

Weber, Jeff. "The Roles Of Allies, Mentors And Sponsors In Employee Development." September 27, 2019. Retrieved from https://www.forbes.com/councils/forbeshumanresourcescouncil/2019/09/27/the-roles-of-allies-mentors-and-sponsors-in-employee-development/.

World Economic Forum. "Future of Job Reports 2025." January 7, 2025. Retrieved from https://reports.weforum.org/docs/WEF_Future_of_Jobs_Report_2025.pdf.

Wronski, L. & Cohen, J. "A third of US workers seriously considered quitting their job in the last 3 months. Here's why." CNBC. July 16, 2019. Retrieved from https://www.cnbc.com/2019/07/16/third-of-us-workers-considered-quitting-their-job-in-last-3-months.html.

Zheng, W., Kim, J. Kark, R., & Mascolo, L. "What Makes an Inclusive Leader?" Harvard Business Review. September 27, 2023. Retrieved from https://hbr.org/2023/09/what-makes-an-inclusive-leader.

www.ingramcontent.com/pod-product-compliance
Lightning Source LLC
Chambersburg PA
CBHW070614030426
42337CB00020B/3800